PRAISE FOR

When You Shake the Family Tree

"This book is a prime example of how sharing one's story with powerful vulnerability can deeply impact others. Margo's storytelling captured me from the first word, and her compassionate heart benefits everyone lucky enough to learn from it."

—**ELIZABETH LYONS**, author of
Write the Damn Book Already

"Margo Reilly's *When You Shake the Family Tree* is a profound exploration of generational patterns and the power to break them. With raw honesty and deep insight, Reilly unpacks her family history, revealing the inherited traumas that have shaped her life and others', while offering a road map for healing and change. This courageous memoir is proof that we can be cycle breakers."

—**KIM STROBEL**, speaker, author, educator, and happiness coach

"*When You Shake the Family Tree* is a riveting unraveling of family secrets and lies that lead to a powerful rewriting of the self. This book is a must-read for anyone who wants to disrupt generational patterns and choose, as Reilly does, 'It stops with me.'"

—**CINDY CHILDRESS**, PhD, ghostwriter and co-author of *The Logical Law of Attraction*

"This is one of the most courageous memoirs, steeped in Margo's faith, trust in her intuition, and courage to discover the true story of her lineage. This book will keep you on the edge of your seat and encourage you to dig deep into your self and soul for the truth and answers you've been seeking. You will not be able to put this transformative book down and will not come away as the same person."

—JULIE REISLER, intuitive coach, author, mentor, and host of *The You-est You* podcast

"*When You Shake the Family Tree* is the story of Reilly's experience after learning the truth surrounding her paternity. This DNA surprise, occurring when Reilly was in her fifties, was emotionally complex since her biological dad had lived across the street from the author during her youth. She knew his sons (her half brothers) throughout her life as well as her biological grandparents, now deceased. This discovery pushed Reilly into an existential labyrinth in which she sought to reorient her self-perception. The author grieved what might have been, knowing that her abusive childhood and dysfunctional sibling relationships were in stark contrast to those of the normal family to whom she was close both physically and by blood. This book allows the reader to join the author as she journeys toward healing. Anyone affected by a DNA surprise or a hidden family secret will appreciate Reilly's candid sharing of the emotional turbulence that followed once she uncovered the truth."

—JENNIFER E. HASSEL, author of *Badass Grief: Changing Gears, Moving Forward*

"This powerful second book and sequel Margo Reilly has written is a profoundly brave account of the deep exploration she was willing to do for herself and through her desire to be instrumental in generational healing. This act of love and self-healing will have a great impact on both her loved ones and you, the reader, to face what is and transform your own life.

"As for the story, I was on the edge of my seat! Truth is stranger than fiction, and the truths Margo shares with you in the telling of her story and her family's story are well worth the read. Find out what happens when you dare to shake the family tree."

—DR. MICHELLE BARR, author of *Loving What's Next: What You Want Can Be Yours Now!*

"*When You Shake the Family Tree* is a fascinating account of Margo's self-exploration through DNA to discover her longing for an understanding of who she is. Margo's ability to recapture her experience for the reader is [a testament to] her talent as a writer and communicator. Her ability to be vulnerable with herself and entrust the reader with her raw, naked truth of her experiences and gained wisdom to impart hope to others is sheer kindness to the world. A journey of self-exploration is a must for all of us as a way to heal ourselves and the world. Margo's ability to explain her process and the full circle leading back to looking to herself to heal is life changing. Margo teaches radical acceptance of life as hopeful expectations lead to disappointment and a full circle of looking to oneself."

—KRISTIN HAMMOUD, author of *What Is Wrong with Me?*

When You Shake the Family Tree:
Untangling the Roots of True Identity Through DNA

by Margo Reilly

© Copyright 2024 Margo Reilly

ISBN 979-8-88824-678-8

All rights reserved. No part of this publication may be reproduced, stored in a retrieval system, or transmitted in any form or by any means—electronic, mechanical, photocopy, recording, or any other—except for brief quotations in printed reviews, without the prior written permission of the author.

Elizabeth Lyons, Initial Editor

Published by

3705 Shore Drive
Virginia Beach, VA 23455
800-435-4811
www.koehlerbooks.com

WHEN YOU SHAKE
THE FAMILY TREE

WHEN YOU SHAKE THE FAMILY TREE

*Untangling the Roots of
True Identity Through DNA*

Margo Reilly

VIRGINIA BEACH
CAPE CHARLES

This book is dedicated to my beautiful grandchildren. Their birth and existence are the only proof I'll ever need that the love we give will always find its way back to us.

And to the seekers like me who are out in search of themselves. May you find comfort and connection in my story.

"In order to love who you are, you cannot hate the experiences that shaped you."

—ANDREA DYKSTRA

CONTENTS

Introduction 1

PART 1: THE WOUND 5

   Chapter 1: Be Careful What You Wish For 7

   Chapter 2: The Truth Shall Set Us Free 17

   Chapter 3: You've Got Mail 26

   Chapter 4: If Clouds Could Talk 34

PART 2: OPENING THE WOUND 43

   Chapter 5: The Sound of Crickets 45

   Chapter 6: The Tangled Web 55

   Chapter 7: Photographs 64

   Chapter 8: Breaking the Ice 72

   Chapter 9: History Repeats Itself 79

   Chapter 10: The Last to Know 87

   Chapter 11: The Power of a Book 95

   Chapter 12: Rejection Is Protection 105

PART 3: HEALING THE WOUND 113

   Chapter 13: Signs and Synchronicities 115

   Chapter 14: Family Secrets 123

   Chapter 15: The Way Out Is In 131

   Chapter 16: Be the Person You Seek 139

   Chapter 17: Grieving What You Never Had 148

Epilogue	154
Appreciation	158
Resources	160

INTRODUCTION

Patterns. They are everywhere. Literally everywhere. Your morning routine and habits. The way you act around certain people. The way an engine ignites a car. Patterns are nothing more than predictable repetitions, essentially the foundation of all things. They steer the brick-and-mortar construction of houses and buildings. They even determine our DNA coding. And they are effortlessly guiding the outcomes of our lives, more than we likely could ever know.

I became privy to the patterns of life when I began to dissect my family history under a magnifying glass and quickly discovered some recurring themes. History was repeating itself over and over in my family's book of life. It was blatantly obvious. No need to even dig deep.

I had written my first memoir, *When the Apple Falls Far from the Tree*, as a nurturing gift to myself in order to heal the "mother wound" I had dealt with throughout my life. I had no realization while writing that book that what I was truly uncovering was much larger. I had many wounds: A mother wound. A father wound. A sibling wound. A family wound.

It wasn't until the book was published and in the hands of readers that I had this great epiphany. I was enlightened to the fact that my family cycles or patterns would, in fact, continue to repeat themselves over and over and over again until someone or something decided it was time to disrupt them. To halt the repetitive experiences occurring within each new generation's lifetime. The result was a call to action.

While some themes passed down from one generation to the next are welcome, many are not. There are a multitude of reasons for this, of course, the most obvious being that as time goes on and we begin to "know better," we should ultimately want to "do better" for our people. For our loved ones.

My story will highlight the fact that many families are oblivious to the reality of "history repeating itself" within their construct. They partake in keeping patterns alive and thriving, feeding them without knowing they exist. Often, even when they do know, they neither heed nor comprehend the damage they could be instilling in yet another generation of family members. Understandably, turning a blind eye and ignoring these truths often seems the easier, more acceptable route.

When thinking of the things passed down from one generation to the next, we can immediately turn to traits like eye and hair color, career paths, nicknames, wealth, and even geographical location. We may automatically contemplate traditions that surround celebrations, such as birthdays, holidays, and various religions. Rarely do we think of the possible ramifications of mental and physical health patterns playing out in current or upcoming generations. The power of social/emotional patterns also becomes clear if we are brave enough to trace our roots through the hands of time. When and if we do, we may find proof of a recurring theme of generational trauma, a pattern we should get curious about. A pattern we have the power to disrupt if we so choose.

According to allpointsnorth.com, "Experts describe generational trauma as post-traumatic effects that aren't just experienced by one person, but are handed down, like an unwanted legacy, from one generation to the next. Anything about the traumatic event may be passed down, from the memories and stories about the event itself, to the more subtle and insidious ways in which the trauma has affected both the person directly involved and the family."

If you were to research generational trauma, you would find that scientists have proven that trauma is stored in the body and passed down through our DNA. It exists deep in the tissues of who we are. It's part of our genetic makeup, a blueprint of sorts.

For me, this discovery meant that I was chosen to break the cycle. To change my family's DNA. To begin the healing process by halting generational patterns and experiences that are unhealthy and of no benefit to the people I love. I had been living with the weight of decades of emotional baggage that didn't even belong to me. The time had come for me to make a clear and conscious decision to draw a line in the sand—a hard line, proclaiming that it stops with me. That my children would not be next in line to carry on these insidious, embedded ways of coping with and navigating a life of dysfunctional family ties.

Watching the same themes plague yet another generation was simply too painful for me to ignore. As the black sheep of the family, I certainly had nothing to lose and only a hopeful, more peaceful future to gain. Just saying, "It stops here" out loud instantly made my body and mind feel expansive, liberated.

Understanding terms like *generational trauma*, *re-parenting*, and *cycle breaking* has become part of my daily life. It is my mission to learn and address them to my fullest potential in the years to come and then share them with anyone else who also seeks to heal their roots. If I stop even one unwanted trauma from repeating itself, I have done my job. If I help inspire you to do the same, I am even more grateful for this quest bestowed upon me.

I proudly confess that it was sobriety from alcohol that allowed me to awaken to this understanding, this mission. It was the beginning of the growth and change that continues to happen inside of me, a metamorphosis that has no ending. I have committed myself to this work for the remainder of my days. It is my hope and intention that my daughters will take note and carry on the tradition of cycle breaking instead of bearing the burden of dysfunction. While every family has it to some degree or another, I want them to know they have the power to change family dynamics. And I want you to know that you can, too.

My first memoir provides a great foundation for the reading of this book. But it may also be interesting to start here and then travel back to see how the story actually began.

You are now embarking on the story of how I discovered who I am on an even deeper level than my sobriety journey brought about. The unveiling of a more profound sense of self. This continued self-discovery began after some intentional soul searching uncovered a hidden truth about the physical me. The human me.

I have forever been agitated by the phrase "It runs in the family." As if it were simply fact. A life sentence with no room for change.

Yes, it runs in my family. And I've decided this is where it runs out.

—Margo Reilly

PART 1

The Wound

> There's been a never-ending battle,
> Between what I feel and what I know,
> The stubborn voice of reason,
> Against a heart that won't let go,
> So I sat instead to listen,
> To what was in my soul,
> It told me not to dwell on things,
> That are out of my control.
>
> Christie L. Starkweather

CHAPTER 1

Be Careful What You Wish For

When I wrapped up writing my first memoir, it felt like I'd settled on an appropriate ending. A conclusion to some truly epic chapters that had finally settled down enough that I could pick through the pieces and make tangible meaning of my life thus far. I hadn't a single clue that the ending of that book would evoke the beginning of the next one. My life has been one giant roller coaster ride, and it turned out it was time for another unexpected twist and perilous tunnel.

In the opening chapter of *When the Apple Falls Far from the Tree*, I referenced a memoir I was reading at the time, written by author Jamie Kern Lima. She shared her emotional experience of accidentally learning that she had been adopted. She was blindsided and in disbelief, but I couldn't relate to her disappointment. There were many, many times in my younger years when I wished quite hard for a different family. More times than I care to recount. I had no idea then that there would come a day when similar news arrived to rock my own world—but it did.

"I want all of you to imagine a doctor has just walked into the room. He or she informs you that you only have twenty-four hours to live. Now take your writing journals and jot down what your top three regrets would be if you found out you were leaving this lifetime tomorrow. I am setting the timer for five minutes. Start writing," she ordered.

I grabbed my closest pen and scratched at the paper easily. I don't have huge regrets, per se, but there were longings inside of me for certain. Things my soul would need in order to be fulfilled when my life came to an end. It's fair to say that, ironically, my recent recovery from alcohol dependency had created a personal-development addiction of sorts. I couldn't get enough of learning and understanding more about myself and the ways of the universe. I had adopted a thirst to feel and process all that was happening to me. Within me.

I deep-dived into an online personal growth course with life coach Sheri Salata. A midlifer who played right hand to Oprah for years as her executive producer, Sheri has witnessed more than a few incredible things. Sitting in her front-row seat at Harpo Studios, she has heard and learned from many gurus. And this beacon of hard-truth telling and pillar of motivation was now coaching and spreading the wisdom she had collected all those years, front and center. I wanted to up my growth game, and without hesitation I paid a few shiny pennies to sign up for her ninety-day online excavation course.

We were completing the above-mentioned writing prompt, which she referred to as her "green plaid couch" journaling exercise, via Zoom. The idea for this thought-provoking activity came about after she shared a deep conversation with her dying mother on their family couch. There were about fifty attentive faces on the screen, intently listening to her words and following her specific directions.

As the timer chimed and we concluded our writing, she advised us to look down at what we had written. She then directed us to pick one of those three dying regrets (or longings, in my case) and make a stand to do something about it, right then. Our task was to choose one for which we could gain momentum almost immediately. I knew without hesitation which one it was and made a heartfelt commitment to myself. A promise that I would take action directly after that session ended.

I looked down at my paper, at the inked handwriting that resembled my mother's, and read the line out loud to myself: "I don't want to die without knowing if my father is really my father."

Could I take immediate action toward ending this yearning? Of course I could. At-home DNA kits are insanely cheap, reliable, and easily obtainable. A test that wasn't possible a mere decade ago is now as accessible as a pregnancy test.

It was late in the evening when our virtual class ended during that summer of 2021, but I still decided to text my oldest brother, Eric, right then, as Sheri had instructed.

"Hey. Huge favor to ask. Would you be willing to do an Ancestry test if I paid for it? I want to find out if Dad is in fact my dad or not."

"I don't know," he texted back promptly.

I dialed his number, since he seemed available, and began to explain my intention to find out whether we were whole or half siblings. There was no denying he was my dad's son. They were too much alike in so many ways, and he knew this, too.

I let him know that at-home DNA kits also provided lineage details, something I knew would pique his interest as a historian. I hoped it would be the selling point in convincing him to help me out. I told him I would purchase the two kits, and with little hesitation, he agreed.

When our tests arrived a week or so later, I was excited to finally be doing something about this internal itch that had made its way to the surface. I dutifully spit into the provided vial and sealed it up to send off for examination. I had to giggle at the contrast between the two boxes awaiting pickup from our favorite UPS guy. One was headed to the Ancestry lab so that my DNA details could be determined. The other contained my feces sample—an at-home screening kit my doctor had given me for colon cancer indicators. I teased the driver about the importance of making sure my bodily secretions made it safely to the right labs. *My goodness,* I thought. *Crazy to think about what is exchanged via cardboard packages these days!*

I dropped my brother's kit off at his house a day or two later, and he sent in his saliva sample about a week after I had sent mine.

A confirmation email soon arrived, stating that the results should take six to eight weeks. I did my best during that time to forget about the whole idea. But the Ancestry website's process would not allow for that to happen. It seemed I was receiving daily notifications.

"We received your kit."

"We're processing your kit."

"Our experts are working hard on your DNA."

So much for putting it out of my mind! Waiting on those results began to consume me, those bits of seductive correspondence each day enticing me to remain anything but calm.

On an ordinary evening, far sooner than the suggested six-to-eight-week time frame, an email notification popped up on my laptop as I browsed aimlessly. It was August 29, 2021, just a couple of days before I would return to the classroom to attend teacher training for the school year ahead. It was around eight o'clock, and I was home alone, watching television, comfy in my pajamas. I got rather excited when I read the notification on my screen: "Your Ancestry results are ready!"

In hindsight, I wish it had also come with a flashing warning light and encouragement to grab a support person. Some bold words, perhaps "Proceed with caution." However, there was no such forewarning about what would transpire once I clicked the hyperlink that would irrevocably open doors to a world different from the one I'd been comfortably sitting in moments before.

I clicked on the notification without hesitation. Even though it arrived sooner than expected, I had waited long enough.

I was directed to the Ancestry website. The many tabs and options to choose from made it confusing to know where to begin. The first subtitle to catch my eye was "Your DNA Story." I hastily double-clicked to get the answers I was seeking. I knew that it should take at least another week or two for my brother to obtain his information. But I was eager to see what had already been calculated for me in the portal.

The web page I arrived on displayed a map and a pie chart, confirming that I am mostly European, half-Polish and half-Irish. This wasn't news to me; I had expected to find this. Though I did wonder where my German roots were. My dad had always prided himself on his German heritage. There was no German descent showing in the results, but I was educated enough to know that it was possible my dad was misinformed about pieces of his family lineage. I decided there was nothing interesting or surprising enough to keep me scrolling on that particular page.

Then I saw a tab labeled "Your DNA Matches."

My DNA matches? What does that mean? I wondered. *My brother's results couldn't possibly be in yet. Has someone else from my family already submitted a kit?* Turns out, that was exactly the case, though I hadn't so much as entertained the possibility. Up until that moment, I'd been focused solely on the results from my brother and me, on whether we would be a full sibling match.

Duh, I realized. *Of course, other people have taken this test!* I clicked in hurried curiosity. *Matches? What a bonus this feature is!*

A never-ending list of names began to populate the screen of my computer. First cousins, second cousins, distant cousins, and so on. At the very top was my first cousin Jennifer. My mom's sister's daughter. I recalled that she had mentioned taking the test some time ago.

But I couldn't focus on her name whatsoever because of the name listed in the second row on the screen, just below hers. A name that would flip my world upside down the instant my eyes met it. My jaw dropped heavily in amazement. My eyes bulged from their sockets. My heart was beating fast and hard against my chest. I went entirely numb, no longer in control of my body parts. The truth of my existence was confirmed in that split second. The twelve-inch laptop cradled atop my legs displayed the answer to a lifelong burning question. I could barely make my fingers click the buttons on my phone. I felt confused, like I was on heavy drugs. I needed my husband. I needed him immediately.

The only words to come out of my mouth when he answered were "Hurry home. My Ancestry results are in."

He was just minutes away and would thankfully walk through our door a few minutes later. He knew this could get interesting, and he approached our living room with genuine curiosity. He found me frozen, unable to move a limb, laptop still perched on my thighs. I slowly turned the screen so he could see what my eyes were glued upon, and together, we connected the first of many dots.

I couldn't tell if my world was being turned upside down or tilted right side up. It felt as if both were happening at the exact same time. Nausea set in, and I thought I might throw up all over the electronic device that had just unveiled my truest, most authentic identity.

You see, a little birdie had once told me a story. Actually, it wasn't a little birdie at all. It was my very drunken mother.

If you read my first memoir, you already know that she seemed to enjoy inflicting pain on others. When I was a young girl, about eleven years old, she spewed some extremely harsh words at me, words I would never forget. We were deep in an argument, and I told her that I was going to leave her crazy house to finally go live with my dad.

With cruel intent she shouted back, "Your father probably isn't even your real father."

Her words passed through my ears, and at the time I didn't give them any credibility. She often spat out hurtful things to be spiteful, so this was nothing unusual. It was easy enough to ignore what she had so carelessly said, especially since it was pointless for a little girl to argue with a highly intoxicated, narcissistic adult.

When I attempted to bring this up the following day, she denied we'd had the conversation. As if I'd made the whole thing up. That is what narcissists do. Make you believe that you are the crazy one. Perhaps she truly didn't remember saying it to me. It was in the heat of the moment, and she was fairly lit from drugs and alcohol. For whatever reason, I gave up and didn't press it any further with her. It was never brought up again.

That moment in time, however, became the shelter for a buried curiosity I would carry with me from that point on. I spent decades pondering this potential truth in the back of my mind.

She is a compulsive liar, I convinced myself anytime the thought returned.

But what if? I would wonder simultaneously.

As a young child, I did not know how to process this information or whether I should give any merit to what she blurted out that day. She was always embellishing her stories, and I wanted to believe this was just another of her crazy moments of lashing out to hurt me and rob me of my power. But when she lashed out that day, she also gave me a name. A name I was somewhat familiar with. One that was, in that moment, branded on my psyche.

I didn't know the man personally. But I did know most of his family. In fact, his son and nephew, who were around my age, would become my friends in adolescence. I can remember half-jokingly saying to them in our early teenage years at a party, "Hey, I might be related to you." We never investigated or even fully understood what this actually implied. We were babies who didn't have a care in the world about the importance or significance of genetics.

I had also recognized the name because my potential father's family lived right across the street from my paternal grandparents when I was growing up. The kind of neighbors that present more like family. The front porches of these two households lined up in perfect parallel on the tiny street that divided their houses. My grandmother, who raised me during my teenage years, had always spoken of this family with adoration and kindness.

The curiosity brewing inside me for all those years finally came to light. It was no longer a mere possibility. I was not my father's biological child, something I had innately known all along but was equally in denial of.

On that evening in August 2021, my whole entire life suddenly made complete sense.

No, I cannot say I was fully blindsided by this nugget of truth, because the seed had been planted decades before. But there was most certainly a feeling of shock pulsing through me now that I knew the absolute truth. Now that I understood what it meant.

DNA doesn't lie, my thoughts affirmed again and again.

My emotions shot all over the place and quickly landed on a surge of validation. A gut instinct that I had always felt tugging deep inside had now been factually proven. My intuition had served me well. No more curiosity about a possible truth. There was no denying it any longer. It was right there in front of me in black and white. Spelled out crystal clear across my little laptop screen.

Still numb with shock, I dialed my brother.

"Hey, what's up?" he mumbled on the other end. We don't talk all that often, so he knew there must be a reason for the late-evening call.

"My test results just came in. Guess what? She was telling the truth. Dad is not my biological father. And guess what else? A ton of Robert Reilly's family members are linked up to my tree."

My brother was hesitant in his reaction but also not in denial.

"DNA doesn't lie," we concluded.

He was my half brother. I have no full siblings. I have two half brothers from my mother. And two newly acquired half brothers from my biological father's side. It was difficult to wrap my head around this. But the pebble had been cast. The ripple effect had been set in motion.

It would be impossible to explain the plethora of emotions that ran through me in such a short amount of time. I was up, down, all around. I wanted to scream and cry and laugh all at once. My mind and body felt altered. Taken over.

On one hand, I was thankful that my inner compass had kept me curious all those years. Something deep inside always hinted toward this truth. But I also held instant pity for the father who had a hand in trying to raise me. He'd had so much disappointment throughout his life.

Could he possibly know? I suddenly thought. *Is this why we have never had any sort of decent relationship?* Anger scratched its way to the surface at this thought. What if this secret, retained by one or possibly both of my parents, had kept me from a totally different life? A better life? I had survived a horrific childhood, after all.

During this moment of unraveling, I was grateful for all the personal-growth work I had done over the last few years. I began to understand that it was the prerequisite to finding my truth. I would not let my erratic yet justifiable emotions take me over for too long.

Breathe, girl. Deep breaths here, I instructed myself repeatedly.

I had to set my thinking straight. My confirmation of truth was all-consuming. It was almost too much to manage as a freshly sober woman.

I was no accident. I was on purpose. I was absolutely meant to be. Everything up to this point in my life had prepared me for this day of self-discovery. That moment, right then, was when the truth was meant to be uncovered. It was divine timing, and I knew I would need to completely trust in its unfolding.

The spiritual part of me wondered if my mother had given me a nudge from the "other side." Telling me it was time to put an end to the curiosity that had plagued me for so many years. Perhaps it was time to stop looking in the mirror and wondering exactly who that person in the reflection was. While I knew wholeheartedly that it was always my inner soul looking back, I could now make sense of my physical features, too.

It was getting quite late into the night, but there was not an ounce of sleep to be had that evening. Bedtime instead became a whirlwind of questions and scenarios playing out erratically in my head. I could not help but predict what this discovery would do to all parties involved but did my best to refocus on myself.

I did nothing wrong here. This was not my fault. I echoed this over and over. I also speculated about what this new information was meant to do for me. *Why now? What does it all mean? Will anything even change? What do I do with this information now that I know who I really am?*

The long night blurred seamlessly into the next day. The day I would step out of my bed and get ready in my bathroom mirror as a completely different person.

My reflection was almost too much to take in.

> The truth won't set us free—
> until we develop the skills
> and the habit
> and the talent
> and the moral courage
> to use it.
>
> *Margaret Heffernan*

CHAPTER 2

The Truth Shall Set Us Free

They say the truth shall set us free. But first it's going to fuck us up a little bit.

The next several days felt surreal. Something out of a television show. Like an out-of-body experience where I was split from myself, looking down on my body, robotically going through the motions. The motions of pretending that nothing had happened when, in fact, I was no longer the person I was the day before. There were moments I felt like I was going out of my mind, like this couldn't possibly be happening in real life. There were episodes where I cried so hard that there were no tears left to shed. There were instances where my mind would abruptly step in and try to convince me that this was no big deal at all.

But it was a big deal. It's still a big deal! My identity and assumed genetic makeup had changed right before my eyes. This new knowledge felt so permanent. Irreversible. Unfathomable.

While I may not have been 100 percent blindsided by this news, I still had to process the sheer reality of it. I was not prepared for this roller coaster ride, even if I had purposefully brought it upon myself. So many questions ran rampant, and there were only three people who could answer them to the best of their knowledge: my mother, who was now deceased; my birth certificate (BC) father, who I was no longer on speaking terms with; and the man who was actually responsible for creating my life yet likely didn't know it.

Decisions, decisions.

I decided to first reach out to one of my "new" half brothers, Paul. The one I joked with about our possible connection in those earlier adolescent years. He was still in the circle of friends my husband and I shared here in our hometown, and I wanted to let him know that I had finally uncovered the truth. I knew he would be kind and accepting of the news, so I typed a brief message and sent it out with high hopes. I needed to confess to him that the little joke I obliviously shared all those years ago was actually a fact.

Hey there!

Hope all is well. I feel like it's been ages since I saw you last!

I wanted to let you know that I did an official Ancestry DNA test. Yesterday evening I got the results back. And lo and behold, I am a Reilly. Many matches showed up on the Reilly side as well as your grandma Doris's side.

I will admit I'm not surprised at all and feel I have always known deep down inside.

I'm letting you know because all of these people that are connected to Ancestry are going to get an email stating that I have been connected to their family tree. Your cousin Leanne already knows, and I see there are several others who have also "viewed" this new addition to the DNA family tree. (So some people may inquire. Or perhaps keep it to themselves, who knows?)

I don't plan to do anything with this information as of now. I just had a deep-seated longing to know who I was.

I didn't want you to be blindsided if something were to come up in conversation.

Most importantly, I hope you understand that I needed to do this for myself.

❤ Margo

Paul is a sweet guy, five or six years older than me. I expected him to be gentle with the news, and he didn't let me down.

He replied a short time later that same day.

> Margo, I always had the same feeling. I totally understand your need to know and I'm glad you have the answer. If you ever decide you want to talk to my dad, let me know and I would gladly break the ice with him. I look forward to seeing you guys sometime soon. Love ya, sis!

His words meant the world to me during the upheaval this discovery caused. I was feeling untethered. Torn. Conflicted. But his acceptance felt promising and comforting. Brotherly. Don't get me wrong; I knew full well that he might be the only one in that family to embrace me. But it made me feel more hopeful to know that at least one person had compassion for a situation that stemmed from a decision made decades earlier. Something completely out of my control. If he could find it within himself to be forgiving and understanding, maybe the others in his family unit would follow suit.

Our text conversation continued, and we eagerly decided to meet up in the coming days. I wanted to show him precisely what had populated my computer screen in hopes that he could help me connect some of the dots. It took me a day or two to navigate the Ancestry website and figure out who was showing up from my maternal bloodlines versus who was there because of my new paternal discovery. The website now has the capability to do that for you automatically. But in 2021, that feature wasn't yet available.

Paul was very understanding and welcoming in his responses. I found solace in knowing he had believed in our possible kinship since the day I suggested it. He confessed that I resemble his aunt, which made him believe it was a very real possibility.

Paul had volunteered as tribute, bravely stating that he would be the one to go to his dad, Robert, with this information. We both agreed it would be best if Robert learned this truth privately, before members of his family began to ask how or why I was connecting to their trees on Ancestry. The site did not outright state who my father was. But if you clicked around and did the slightest bit of investigation, it wouldn't be hard to draw a conclusion. His parents were displayed as my paternal grandparents due to the connections of common relatives.

As a few weeks passed following my conversation with Paul, it became clear that I'd need to be the one reaching out. The news should come directly from me. After all, this was my revelation, not Paul's. My own research and discovery was about to abruptly rock Robert Reilly's world, and I didn't want to burden or trouble anyone else with the unfolding of my personal story. I thanked my brother for his willingness to participate and assured him that I would take responsibility for sharing the news from this point forward.

I decided to type a letter. A good old-fashioned note that would arrive in Robert's mailbox. A surefire way for me to express everything I wanted to say in an eloquent yet matter-of-fact manner. Able to share my findings and feelings without interruption or question, I effortlessly poured my heart onto the pages, hoping to represent the person I had become. My intention was pure. There was no blaming or shaming.

The words flowed as if that moment had been written in the stars. I had no feelings of regret or doubt, only confidence and certainty. This was how it was meant to unfold. I proofread my writing several times, then shared it with my husband and daughters to get their opinions. Everyone agreed that it was friendly and to the point, and I just needed to mail it before I talked myself out of it.

I dropped the letter in the outgoing mail at our local post office on my way to work the next morning. I used two stamps just in case the three pages inside the envelope required extra postage. I didn't want anything to hinder its prompt delivery to his home address, only thirty miles down the road from me.

Even after mailing it, I must have read it over and over on my screen a hundred times, each time thinking of him and how he would react to the words he'd absorb once he opened it.

10/10/21

Dear Robert,

I realize that receiving this letter is nothing short of awkward and surprising, but I hope you will read on from start to finish so that you can understand my need to send it to you.

My name is Margo, and I am your biological daughter.

I know it is possible you have heard rumors about this many moons ago, but I have now confirmed this truth through Ancestry DNA testing.

I guess it is fair to say, I have spent most of my life with an inner knowing about this truth. When I was young, around 11 or 12, my mother revealed that you could potentially be my biological father when she was very intoxicated. I asked her further questions the next day, but she denied we had any sort of conversation and would not speak of it again. She passed away this past spring, so I cannot go to her for answers surrounding the truth of my existence.

Knowing and now confirming this truth is perplexing to say the least. Nothing is different, yet everything has changed. I am a Reilly. Your Irish bloodlines make up half of who I am.

I don't recall you from my youth. But I do recall many of your family members. Your father, Max, was very sweet to me when I was so young. Spending time with me on his or my grandmother's front porch. Giving me money to buy ice cream or pizza with my friends. I cannot help but wonder if he had an innate sense that I might have belonged to his family.

I remember finding a picture of you once. I sought it out to kill my curiosity. I must have been in my early twenties.

I looked at the picture and instantly knew that we shared DNA. It was like looking into a mirror and seeing my own reflection. I have spent the past years of my life tucking that knowing deep down inside.

But I cannot unknow this truth any longer. Much of my life has been estranged on and off from both of my parents, who led toxic and unstable lives. I have always questioned my sense of belonging. Just recently, I convinced my oldest brother to complete DNA kits with me so that I could put this feeling to rest. As you may have predicted, he connected to members of his family, while I found myself staring at many of your ancestors and family members listed on my family tree. Not only did it confirm that my brother and I were "half" siblings, it also confirmed that Leanne and I had grandparents in common and that she was a first cousin to me through DNA matching.

I am informing you because I do not plan to keep my true identity a secret. I have already shared my findings with my immediate family and close friends and will somehow, someday, let my father know that I have confirmed what I was told so many years ago. It will certainly be hard for him to hear, but something also tells me he is not going to be surprised. We have never had any sort of normal father/daughter relationship, and I can't help but wonder if it is because maybe, deep inside, he has always felt this truth as well.

I sympathize with the shock of this news for all involved. However, I hope you can understand that I need to do this for myself. For my daughters. We all need and deserve to know where we come from regardless of the circumstances in which we were created. That is now history, after all.

While my mother led a rather sad and unstable existence, please know that I myself am very successful, considering my traumatic childhood. I have been a schoolteacher for the past 22 years, I married my high school sweetheart, and I have two wonderful grown daughters. We reside in your hometown and have all our lives. We know many of your family members personally, including your sons.

I understand it will take some time to process this news. I know you have a wife, and I hope she too will be compassionate about this situation. Please take the time you need. I do not have intentions of interrupting or upsetting your life. But I am curious . . . and would love the chance someday to sit down face-to-face and perhaps discuss family history, etc.

I realize full well it may turn out that you do not have the same curiosities that I do. If you do not wish to meet or know me in any capacity, I respect that is your decision. I can gather information about my lineage in other ways. I just need you to be aware that I am actively searching for "who I am" and the roots I stem from.

I am including a few photographs from over the years. Perhaps you will see the resemblance as well.

I hope, in response, to receive some sort of correspondence to let me know you have in fact received and read this letter. And how you would like to proceed forward so that I can respect your wishes. This, of course, after you have taken ample time needed to digest this news.

Sincerely,
Margo

I was certain to include all the possible ways he could respond and get in touch with me. I gave my phone number. My email. My home address.

And then the real waiting began. I braced myself for both the best- and worst-case scenarios. My mind busily played out all the potential ways this news could go down. I worried whether or not the letter would arrive safely. I regretted not sending it "certified" so that I would have confirmation of delivery to his address. All this wondering, dreaming, and worrying quickly became torture, and I prepared to wait a long time.

    I am delighted to report that I did not have to wait long at all.

> Our willingness to wait
> reveals the value we place
> on the object
> we are waiting for.
>
> Charles Stanley

CHAPTER 3

You've Got Mail

It was just after 9 a.m. It was a weekday, so I was at school, tending to my class of little humans. We were in the gymnasium, and as I cheered my students on to run their laps and increase their heart rates, I had no idea my own was about to accelerate and join the race.

I glanced down when my smartwatch buzzed to alert me to a notification. Most of the time, I don't even bother to look, as it always seems to be spam or something else of no significance. But on this morning, my eyes met the screen of that watch as though following an order from the divine. *Look down at me. Now.*

There it was in bright-red letters. Bold text across the tiny screen. "Email from Robert Reilly." His name. My biological father's name, staring back at me. Hot blood flooded my face and cheeks. My heart rate skyrocketed. My body turned weightless and floaty. Time stopped. I knew this feeling from a couple of weeks earlier and felt a smile curl across my face. I remember trying to control it. Willing it to stop. *Don't let yourself get excited, Margo!*

I did not expect this. At least, not so soon. I had offered him all the time he needed or wanted to process this news. And here we were, not even a week later, and I was getting a response of some sort. *Does this mean he'll be quick to dismiss me? To tell me that he isn't interested in knowing more about me?*

I knew that I shouldn't read the email until later. But I had been waiting for this opportunity for years. Decades (literally). And the moment called to me like a siren. I quickly got my little ones involved in a fun activity that my classroom aide could supervise, allowing me to grab my phone and view the email in its entirety. I nervously clicked to open the message, hands trembling, soaked in sweat. *Here we go*, I cheered myself on.

The tone of the letter penetrated my heart even before the words met my eyes for consumption. Hopeful vibes elicited a smile that took over my face. I wore the world's biggest grin the entire time I read.

Margo,

Received your letter on Saturday. Shock is still wearing off. I do look forward to meeting you in person. You seem to be a very special person.

    Maybe we can get together privately for coffee or lunch somewhere to talk about the past and where we are heading from here.

    I am sure we both have a lot of questions.

    You can reach me at xxx-xxx-xxxx or at this email address.

Looking forward to meeting you!
Robert

Holy. Shit. He wants to meet me. He seems to be quite curious, too. How the hell am I supposed to go about my day?

This was a major pivot in my life, and I had to do my best to shrug it off for several hours while proceeding to finish out the workday.

I was in utter shock at his response. I'd expected that if I did hear something, the first correspondence might be something along the lines of "I received your letter. Thank you for giving me time to process all of this." But this response, the wording of this response, was almost . . . enthusiastic! Promising. His words did not suggest shame or disbelief, as I had feared. Rather, a sense of openness.

Did he also have a deep-seated knowing this whole time? I wondered.

I willed my body to stop shaking. Gathering myself was an impossible task, but I had to get back to my students and play the role of elementary school teacher for several more hours.

I screenshotted the email and sent it to my husband and daughters in our family group chat. I appropriately titled it "O...M...G," then tucked my phone away and impatiently waited until lunchtime to send a well-considered reply to Robert.

In the hours that I waited to respond, my thoughts surrounding this email consumed me. I couldn't help but picture him sitting across from me, listening to my words as I revealed how long I had speculated about this inevitable truth about the two of us. I envisioned him watching me tell my story while looking for glimpses and proof of himself. I felt confident that meeting me face-to-face would be all the proof he needed.

When lunchtime finally rolled around, I practically sprinted to the teacher lounge. I opened and read the text replies from my family. No surprise, they were excited for me to have this outcome, the one I had sincerely hoped and prayed would happen. A chance to sit and have an actual discussion with this man. The man who helped create me biologically. They, too, expressed that the energy surrounding his response was even better than anticipated.

I sat with my phone in hand at the table to respond to his email. Once again, it felt as though I were floating. In a dream state. I didn't notice a single person or thing around me. I had no appetite and barely touched my food. I remember trying to convince myself to take at least a couple of bites, but the butterflies in my stomach had taken over, and my adrenaline was still pumping as if I'd just opened the email.

What should I say? How should I say it? I didn't want to come off too strong or too desperate. The last thing I wanted to do was spook him. I had his attention and wanted to keep it. I chose my words carefully and vowed to keep it short and simple.

Hi Robert,

I received your email, and I just wanted to let you know that I truly appreciate your willingness to meet and talk. I was hoping for this outcome.

I would love it if just you and I could sit down over some coffee and have a candid conversation together.

I am always out your way for shopping. Let me know your availability and a place where you would feel comfortable to meet up.

I am available evenings and anytime on Saturdays or Sundays.

Let me know what works best for you.

Looking forward,
Margo

Hitting the send button nearly took my breath away. The look on my face must have resembled a kid's on Christmas morning. *Is this really happening? Am I really having a conversation with my biological father?* Caution and excitement collided inside my body.

The human part of me knew not to get my hopes up. I had been let down many times in my life by parent figures. As a child, I battled rejection quite often. I had several firm conversations with myself to get out of my own head, to stop playing out all the potential scenarios that could go down. Yes, things might go great. They could also go seriously south. I had to remind myself that as divinely timed as it all felt, this was only the experience from my side of things. Who knew what was brewing in his thoughts?! Maybe he just wanted to meet and see me one time to let me know that he wasn't interested in any sort of relationship moving forward.

It wasn't necessarily a relationship I was seeking. At least, I didn't believe that to be my motivation at the time. My quest for solving the mystery of my creation was more about acknowledgment. I didn't want to think of myself, my existence, as someone's "dirty little secret." Decades had gone by, and the events that led to my creation could surely be forgiven by now. I needed those involved to come to terms with the truth that I had innately known all this time. I needed them to acknowledge that this was how I came to be.

On the surface, my motivation could be viewed as selfish, I suppose. I was fully aware that the news could upset several families upon being revealed. Robert and I wouldn't be the only ones experiencing the shock. But I would no longer honor this lingering secret on behalf of my parents. I was consciously choosing to lift the veil of shame and free myself, even at the expense of the others involved. The wheels were in motion, and I had to ready myself for whatever repercussions or new beginnings lay in the days ahead. It was a brave move, this I knew for sure, and I deliberately chose to armor up once again.

Those around me weren't afraid to share their opinions on the matter. I have always been an open book, so I candidly told my close friends and family what was happening.

"Oh my god. How could you do that to your father, Margo? You're crazy. I would never be able to do that to my dad!" a close friend said accusingly.

Of course she could not relate. She had been raised by a loving father. Someone who was always there for her. A father figure in every sense of the word. She could not relate to my need to do this because she did not carry or understand the lifetime void felt deep in my bones from the lack of a loving father figure.

Thankfully, I was not looking for approval. I knew exactly what I needed to do. But I also prepared myself for the fact that she would not be the only one who saw what I was doing as too bold to understand.

To be quite honest, it baffled me that anyone would expect me to keep a secret of this magnitude. A secret I didn't choose to be a part of. I hoped Robert wouldn't dare ask this of me when we finally had a chance to meet. In my mind, I rehearsed letting him know, in a polite way, that his secret was no longer a secret. The cat was out of the bag, so to speak. There would be talk. There would be rumors surrounding what was going down between the two of us. I had already stated this in the letter I wrote, and I sincerely hoped he understood I would not be changing my mind. There would not be another day of denying my existence. The past had finally arrived to make itself known to the rest of my future.

There were also many people, including my husband, who were profoundly supportive of my need to go public. This was my story to tell. An integral part of my tale had been revealed, and suddenly everything else I had lived through made total sense. In fact, most people in my close circle were happy to see me make sense of the findings that led me here. I am thankful for their encouragement and motivation to move forward.

The next few days felt long as Robert and I communicated back and forth via email. It was clear he didn't use it often, and I had to practice patience as I waited hours on end for a reply to come through. He had readily provided his phone number in response to my letter, but I wanted to see his face when I heard his voice for the first time. I wanted all of our questions and inquisitions to take place in person, where body language and energy would also be part of the exchange.

At one point in our email conversation, while we were throwing around various locations to meet up, I boldly suggested my own house. Part of me longed for him to see my home, get a glimpse into my life. My haven. My home represents so much about me. This way, he could see firsthand that we were a fairly normal bunch and he had nothing to fear in getting to know us. Maybe, just maybe, he'd suggest coming to his house.

I found myself fantasizing about what his home must look like on the inside. I had nothing to go on, of course. Just the fact that he was retired and he and his wife lived in a lovely suburb outside the big city. I had confirmed this thanks to the advanced technology of Google Maps. I saw the outside of his home and made assumptions about a neat and cozy interior, just like mine.

"How about meeting at a diner just down the road from me called Norma's Kitchen?" he responded.

I took note that he wasn't ready to share the intimacy of a home space at this point. I understood his hesitation, of course, but I also allowed myself a small moment of sadness and disappointment. Meeting at one of our homes could have expedited our way into each other's lives.

I replied and confirmed that the time and place worked fine for me.

I had only three days to wait. It felt like the longest three days of my entire life.

> Before a wound can heal
> it must first be seen.
>
> Julia Cameron

CHAPTER 4

If Clouds Could Talk

It's not every day that a midlife woman meets her biological father at a diner for coffee to chat about the affair that brought her into this world forty-seven years prior. But it was a typical crisp fall day in Western New York. Sunday, October 24, 2021, to be exact. Eight days since my biological father opened my letter announcing he had a daughter.

I couldn't believe I was actually getting into my car to drive out to meet him. This had all happened so fast. Much faster than I had anticipated. I prayed that he would not suddenly change his mind and talk himself out of his decision. Sabotage and gloom fought to win my mind over as I worried frantically that a cancellation would come at any moment. I dutifully tried to stop my negative thoughts from spinning. Perhaps, just like me, he wanted to move forward quickly so he could put an end to his mind racing with endless questions and scenarios.

I confess, my nerves got the best of me that morning. Up until then, I had felt calm and relaxed about reaching out and communicating with him. Like it had been in the cards all along. But that day was different. On that day, I would finally look my truth right in the eye. The butterflies surged in my stomach. Excitement and anxiety tangoed fiercely as I tried hard to convince myself to take deep breaths.

Breathe in, breathe out. Everything is going to be just fine.

What does a grown woman wear when she's going to meet her father for the first time? Even simple decisions felt damn near impossible that morning. I must have torn through half my closet before settling on something simple and comfortable. This was not the time to pick clothing that might make me fuss or fidget. Nerves already promised to help with that.

I hopped in the car and blew my husband a kiss through the window as he watched me roll down our driveway. I wished he were coming with me but also knew this was something I had to do on my own. We stared at each other for a few long seconds as I pulled away, no doubt acknowledging that I would return as a changed woman to some degree.

As I drove along the lakeshore on the way to our meeting place, I couldn't help but notice the sky. The majestic sky has always spoken to me without words, and on this day, I heard it loud and clear. In my rearview, the sky above my house and hometown was dark and gray. Thick, stormy clouds filled the width of my back window. But the view in front of me was quite the opposite. The sky was cracked open, fluffy white clouds sprinkled everywhere, shades of silver blue allowing the most amazing sun rays to shine down on the earth. Down on me. Creating a spotlight that would illuminate my drive.

It made me smile. It was the dawning of a new, beautiful day. Perhaps a new era. Perhaps a new way of being. And I was open to it. This was my sign from the universe. My reminder that it was time to shed what no longer served me and welcome the possibilities. On this brave and uncertain morning, the magnificent sky would be my guide, affirming to me that all was going as planned. *Breathe in, breathe out.*

The GPS on my dashboard warned me that there was only one mile to go. I considered pulling over to the side of the road to take a thoughtful pause, but the warrior in me kept her foot firm on the gas pedal. *We are going to do this. It is time.*

I turned into the parking lot of the diner, which was located in a small shopping plaza. It was busy but not overly crowded, thankfully. As I pulled in, I spotted him and his graying blond hair. He was sitting in his truck, and I felt immediate relief that we would not have to do the awkward handshake inside the restaurant in front of others. I pulled into a parking space two spots away from his.

I took the largest breath I could muster and let it go slowly as I opened the door and stepped out onto the blacktop and into the unknown.

His door opened.

In just seconds, we were gazing into each other's faces. We both wore half smiles as we reached out to awkwardly shake hands. I broke the ice by cracking a joke about not having experienced nerves like that in a long, long time. He shook his head and laughed in agreement.

He looked older than I had expected, though I'm not sure what I was expecting since the man was seventy-two years old. I suppose I held all the images of old photographs in my head. He was casually dressed. Khakis, sneakers, and a light jacket for the crisp fall air. His hair was a mix of blond and gray. I couldn't help but notice he wasn't much taller than I was.

We walked along the sidewalk and through the front doors of the diner. I wondered if he worried someone would recognize him. The hostess told us we were welcome to seat ourselves, and I led us to the only open table, which sat along the big front window. The seats were in the blazing sunlight, so I quickly turned and asked the waitress if anything else happened to be available. The last thing I needed right then was the sun burning down on me like a floodlight. I felt as if I might shake right out of my own skin.

She told us there was a more private booth around back if we were interested, and we nodded without hesitation. Our conversation was sure to turn heads should anybody tune in to what we were about to discuss. I was grateful for this more private option, and I sensed that Robert was a tad relieved too.

We sat across from each other and ordered our coffee. He ordered his black, which I have concluded comes with age. I opened several creamers and a Splenda sweetener as the conversation started. Initially, it felt weird locking eyes. This was certainly one of the most awkward situations I had ever been in, and I could tell he was experiencing the same feelings twenty inches across from me. However, there was no denying it—not that I had any doubt whatsoever. There, two feet in front of me, sat the man responsible for my existence.

I was a replica of him, albeit a female version. The eyes, the nose, the facial features were uncanny. Surely my looks alone must have confirmed this to my mother and the father who raised me over the years of watching me grow. I couldn't get past our resemblance to one another.

I thanked him sincerely for his time. "It means a lot that you agreed to meet me today. To come hear me out."

I imagined how difficult it must have been for him, to have things brought to the surface that he had long since forgotten, most likely on purpose. And to be willing to have such an exchange with a perfect stranger, at that.

One of the first things we spoke of was the letter he'd received in the mail.

"Can I ask what convinced you to meet up with me so quickly?" I asked nervously.

"Well, the letter, of course," he replied. "It was so well written."

I half giggled with a smirk, feeling proud as a peacock at his remark.

"Are you a writer?" he asked.

"Yes. Yes, I am, actually. I just wrote a book. I am an author." A larger smirk planted itself across my face. I'm fairly certain that was the first time I'd said those words out loud and truly believed them. It felt powerful to stake this claim. I was hopeful this would impress him enough to shed any worries that I might be a complete nutcase.

I took note of the sense of success I felt at his compliment and his admission that he had been swayed to reach out because of the compelling words on the page. After all, that was one of the reasons I had written it. To touch his heart and soul, if for only a moment. I confessed that the book I was getting ready to publish was a memoir about my harrowing life experiences thus far. I joked that he needn't worry, since I had finished it before all this Ancestry business went down. I didn't dare share that I was already engaged in writing the book you are currently reading.

I wish I had recorded our conversation so I could capture every word and permanently preserve it. Attempting the replay in my mind is rather difficult. Everything seemed to happen at the speed of light, except for the silent pauses. Those moments felt long—yet welcome. During those moments, we absorbed each other's presence and soaked each other in. It was in this stillness that I got a thorough look at my other half. Aside from our undeniable resemblance, I wondered how similar my mannerisms were to his.

He started with an apology.

"I am really sorry, but I honestly can't recall the details. I just don't remember."

I wondered if that was true. Or if he simply didn't want to remember.

"Margo, those days were quite crazy for all of us. We were partyers. And, well, your mother . . . your mother was . . ." He paused, unable to find the right words.

I interrupted to save him from stumbling.

"There is not a single thing you could say about my mother that I don't already know about. Her ways were known to everyone, even us kids," I assured him.

He seemed relieved that he didn't need to paint the picture for me. For a moment, I allowed my mind to sail back in time. My mother had been an attractive woman in her earlier years. However, she was also quite manipulative and seductive. I pictured her forcing herself on a very drunken man. I wasn't trying to deny his part in this, but I knew her wicked ways and what she was capable of all too well.

I could understand why he would want to forget such an encounter.

I had heard stories about how he was my BC father's neighbor back in the day. He was slightly older than the dad who raised me, but they grew up together as good friends. I decided I wouldn't bring up that factoid for fear of sounding judgmental. Besides, I had already put most of the blame on my promiscuous mother. It was no secret that she "got around," and I am sure my dad's good friends weren't off-limits when it came to what she might have offered when no one was looking.

Robert did not deny having partaken in a one-night stand of sorts, but he claimed he couldn't recall any details of the time frame surrounding it. He stated she had never once mentioned to him the possibility of my being his child. Also, that he'd never heard it from anyone else. It was news to him, and he claimed to have been genuinely blindsided.

I silently questioned whether that was true. My mother wasn't the type to keep her mouth closed about anything. Given that she'd told me in a drunken stupor, there was zero doubt in my mind that she had spoken of the affair to others. Several times, I pictured her arguing with the father who raised me and using it as ammunition to hurt him. She was vicious with her words and often used them to disarm or manipulate others.

This, however, wasn't the time to point fingers and figure out exactly who knew or didn't. It was our first meeting, and it could also potentially be our last. I was grateful for the opportunity to meet this man, and I had to remind myself of that several times as he spoke across the table from me, whenever I felt judgment or confusion trying to take over. I did my best to stay focused and ask pertinent questions. We discussed health history and shared some intimate details surrounding our individual cancer journeys. He also spoke of his mother, my grandmother, dying young from breast cancer. I winced internally, mentally noting that there was now a history of cancer within both my maternal and paternal bloodlines.

There were a couple of times where a long, silent pause would have made for a good time to wrap things up. When I felt that opportunity knock, I quickly conjured up more questions or told more stories to fill the time. I didn't want the conversation to end. As awkward as it was, our conversation had a natural sense of ease about it as well. It was supposed to happen. The two of us were to make our biological connection on this day, and I didn't want to have any regrets about not asking him something that had crossed my mind. This might be the only chance I ever got to put my curiosities to rest.

The waitress checked in on us sporadically. She seemed to pick up on the fact that we were having a rather private conversation and respectfully gave us the space we needed. I was grateful for her quick coffee warm-up every now and then, which also kept things moving at a comfortable pace.

At one point, I excused myself to use the restroom. All that coffee was finally catching up to me and my bladder was no longer letting me ignore it. I immediately regretted my decision to get up, as I knew it could make for a natural place for him to end our conversation. As I returned to the table, I saw I was right to have that concern. Robert had pulled out his wallet and displayed cash at the edge of the table to cue the waitress, and perhaps me, that it was time for us to go. She approached just moments later. I had wanted to offer to pay for our coffee but decided to let him. Any father having coffee with his daughter would, right?

We walked in silence to the front of the diner, where he respectfully held the door open for me. The sun blinded me, and it took a moment to regain my sense of direction and head toward the parking lot. We did not exchange any words as we neared our vehicles. I felt flushed and warm. *Should I shake his hand? Should I lean in to hug him?* I felt instantly nervous as I tried to decide on my approach.

Once we got to my car, I turned to face him, trying my best to take him in. To get a crystal-clear look so as to imprint his every feature into the archives of my brain. I knew that I might never get the chance to look him in the face like that again. I wanted to make the moment last. We both leaned in for a hug and a gentle pat on the back.

"It was nice to meet you," he said with sincerity in his eyes.

"It was nice to finally meet you as well. Thank you for coming here today and for your willingness to chat," I softly uttered back.

We both turned and climbed into our separate vehicles, my hands visibly trembling once again. I peered at the clock on my console. I had lost all sense of time while we were speaking and was amazed that we'd been inside the diner for two hours. It had gone by in a flash. I thought hard about key parts of our conversation, repeating them over and over in my head so none of it would escape my memory.

My immediate instinct was to dial my husband and fill him in on what had transpired. Instead, I paused to ground myself. I wasn't sure if Robert was looking over and waiting for me to pull away first, so I decided to save the conversation with my husband for when I got home. Without turning to see what Robert was doing, I put my car in reverse and exited the parking lot. I was heading home a changed woman. Irreversibly somebody else's daughter.

I granted myself permission to marinate in the silence of the car ride. No music played as my tires hummed down the road. Just me and my deep thoughts as I began to process and unpack all that had just taken place in the cozy corner booth of that diner.

Holy fuck. Did this really just happen?!

PART 2

Opening the Wound

Listen to the silence.
It has so much to say.

Rumi

CHAPTER 5

The Sound of Crickets

When I woke on Monday morning, the day after our meetup, I felt an incredible sense of relief and peace. My chance to look my biological father in the eye and have a full-blown conversation with him was behind me instead of something I would continue to fantasize about for perhaps the rest of my life.

I knew there would be no more correspondence for the time being. No notifications on my phone or smartwatch to spark the adrenaline rush I'd become addicted to over the past few weeks. No more curiosity about what he looked or sounded like. Just another round of "Wait it out" to see if anything else transpired.

The writer in me so desperately wanted to send a thank-you email. Something to state my sincere gratitude for his time and presence on that day. But I decided against it. We had left on good terms. If there was to be any further contact, I wanted it to come from him. I didn't want to be perceived as some crazy lady seeking to fill a void. The ball was in his court, and I urged myself to leave it there. I knew this decision was wise, even if it would be difficult.

I spent some time deep in thought that Monday and surprised myself with my conclusions. I knew with confidence that I was going to be just fine, regardless of whether there was further contact. I knew that just meeting him could be enough. Many others never get that opportunity. I was fortunate that this day had come to fruition for me.

It would no longer be a curiosity festering in my head.

Naturally, I was equally curious, wondering if there could be anything more. Would something grow and develop?

I allowed flashbacks of our conversation to run wild in my head. Mostly, I wondered if he took note of our resemblance. I had always thought I looked just like my mother. But that day in the bustling diner proved me wrong. I look just like him. He is me. The only difference is that he has aged by a couple of decades. At times while we chatted, it was hard to look him straight in the eye because I was so distracted by my reflection looking back at me.

Surely he must be blown away by this too? I wondered if he'd also made this observation and shared it with his wife. I wished I could have read his mind as he drove back home that morning.

It felt good to be at work that day after our meetup. It helped me to busy my mind and stop obsessing about the next email correspondence and whether or not another meetup would happen. I jumped right back into the routine of life and worked hard to shift my focus elsewhere. This was the first day I felt my newfound identity on an entirely different level. It was now deep in my bones. My DNA.

Tuesday morning arrived, and I headed to work after my normal routine. As I was setting up the classroom to get ready for the day ahead, a notification came through. There it was. His name, yet again, staring back at me from my watch face. I had butterflies instantly, the same ones that every other email from him had elicited. I didn't want to be excited or draw conclusions, so I didn't let a smile form on my face just yet. What could this be about? Several possibilities spun through my mind, so I quickly clicked to open and read his words.

Margo,

It was very nice to meet you on Sunday. You have certainly overcome many challenges in your life and turned out to be a terrific person.

I hope you are blessed with good health and prosperity throughout the rest of your life.

You would make any man proud to have as a daughter.

I will be talking to my sons soon and see where we go from here.

Robert

To say I was pleasantly surprised would be an understatement. I truly did not expect this. Tears of excitement and disbelief welled up in my eyes. I was sucked right back into the vortex of overanalyzing everything I possibly could. *Is he thinking about forming a relationship for real?* I hadn't gotten that impression when we left each other at the restaurant. I could tell he was very much still in shock that day. His demeanor was guarded. After all, it had only been eight days since reading my letter. This was all happening so quickly.

But this correspondence most certainly emitted a hopeful tone. A tone that confirmed he was still actively processing everything. And maybe, just maybe, there was a morsel of potential to get to know one another further.

When I got to the sentence that read, "You would make any man proud to have as a daughter," my heart melted. I think I read that line at least five times before moving on to the next. What a sweet thing to say. What an appropriate thing to say. *Could he really tell this about me after just a few cups of coffee?* I agreed with him in my mind, placed my hands on my heart, and thought for just a moment about how he would likely never have the opportunity to know me that deeply. It really was too late for us to ever have that sort of all-knowing bond.

I also clung tightly to the line "I will be talking to my sons to see where we go from here." I understood the urgency of sharing with them. I had already revealed to him that his youngest son knew about me, and so might others in his family, due to Ancestry notifying them of my recent connection to their family tree. I was surprised that he only seemed willing to allow this to move forward if the boys were on board. But I also knew this increased my chances, because of course the boys would accept the situation. One of them had already given the green light! Their easy acceptance could make this all work out somehow.

I wasn't delusional or insensitive. I understood that Robert was coming from a place of shame. After all, I was a dirty little secret—at least, I was way back in 1974 when things initially transpired. I was essentially asking him to embrace his past rather than hide from it. I talked this out several times with my husband. We tried to put ourselves in his shoes and consider how we would react if it were us. The stark reality was, this man had to face his grown children and tell them that they have a sibling who was born while he was still married to their mother. Whether it was nearly fifty years ago or not, it would undoubtedly go down as one of the most awkward conversations someone could have. I wished I could be a fly on the wall. Truly. I wished more than anything to witness this story from all perspectives. I was rather fascinated by its unfolding.

Instead of getting to be a fly in any sense of the word, I would have to settle for crickets. The sound of crickets, that is. To my dismay, days turned into weeks. Weeks turned into a month. I heard absolutely nothing. No updates from Robert or even Paul, whom I had secretly kept informed about our meeting and correspondence.

Could it really be that they haven't connected as a family to discuss this yet? I wondered. *Did the conversation perhaps go south, and my half brother is too sweet to share the bad news with me?*

Something had to be up. I did my best to talk myself off the ledge anytime I found myself visiting it. But when anxiety about my opened can of worms struck, the questions in my head were relentless.

What did he think of me?
What did he tell his wife? Does she want to meet me?
How will he portray me and my intentions when telling his family?
Will I ever hear from him again?
Will anything ever come of this truth?

Has he thought about me each day since our meeting too?
Is life just going to go back to the way it was before I sent the letter?

I wouldn't allow myself to think or believe it was all for nothing. Something deep inside had invoked the courage to write and send that letter. A longing that needed to finally be addressed. That courageous move brought me enormous relief when I found what I had been searching for. A true weight had been lifted after decades of allowing it to bubble deep inside. That alone made all of this well worth it. There would be no regrets. None at all.

But meeting him was only the beginning of a brand-new itch. A curiosity that would no doubt take me over. I was this man's biological daughter. I was made from him, of him. I couldn't help but think of a passage from Dani Shapiro's memoir *Inheritance*, which is about the discovery of her biological father. She had recently learned that she was a donor-conceived child and that she had half siblings. I hung on to every word with the utmost understanding of how she felt.

> Later, it will occur to me that . . . [my biological father] felt, to me, like my native country. I had never lived in this country. I had never spoken its language or become steeped in its customs. I had no passport or record of citizenship. Still, I had been shaped by my country of origin all my life, suffused with an inchoate longing to know my own land.

I attempted to type a message to my half brother Paul several times, each time deleting it and reminding myself that everyone needed time to process this revelation. He would reach out if and when he felt good and ready to share how things had gone down.

My husband also repeatedly reminded me to be patient, something I have never been any good at. My mind had other plans, of course. I convinced myself that several weeks' time could only mean that things didn't go well. Perhaps he had told his sons he was ashamed of himself. Perhaps the half brother I didn't know yet, Tim, had advised him to leave well enough alone and not take this information any further. Maybe the conversation hadn't even happened yet because he was too embarrassed to initiate the topic. "Hey, boys. By the way, you have a sister out there."

My husband suggested that I was disappointed. That I must have been secretly hoping for more than I was letting on.

The truth was, curiosity was killing me. I just wanted to know how the conversation went. Would the exchange be hasty and negative? Or approached gently with compassion and understanding? Did they have the capacity to see it from my point of view? Did they agree that my existence was more significant than a regretful one-night stand?

My answers finally began to trickle in when my husband ran into my oldest biological half brother at a local establishment. The one I was not yet familiar with. The one I hadn't known personally. My husband's friendship with Tim stretched back decades, however, and we'd wondered how things would go the first time they saw each other after the news dropped. I had wanted to be together when this exchange finally took place, but it was not to be.

My new brother greeted my husband with a big hug, handshake, and the words "Hello, brother-in-law."

I had sent my husband a text in preparation for his outing, before this went down. I knew the private party he was attending might have one or both of my two new brothers in attendance. I curiously typed, "Brothers there?" He and I had rehearsed what he would say (in my defense) should a confrontation occur. The response I got back was "Oh, it happened, baby." I literally laughed out loud at his response. I so wanted him to rush home and give me the details, but he had just arrived at the party, so I knew that was not going to happen. Thankfully, a phone call came through about twenty minutes later. I was ecstatic he wasn't making me wait all night for a recap of their conversation.

He said that Tim Reilly was, like his younger brother, accepting of the situation. Tim told my husband that I should expect a "big hug" and a "welcome to the family" when he ran into me for the first time. He shared that regardless of what his father—*our* father—opted to do with this information, it was Tim's intention to get to know me in some capacity.

This was an enormous relief to me. I knew Robert was very concerned about his sons' reactions. Knowing that they were both able to accept this truth and move on from it would be helpful in convincing our father to do the same. It certainly made it less awkward that their parents' union had ended decades earlier. I took comfort that my news was not potentially splitting up a long-standing marriage.

Even if Robert wasn't interested in getting to know me, I felt strongly that a relationship needed to happen for my brothers and me. We were close in age. We lived in the same small city. We went to the same places. And we shared so many friends and acquaintances. It only made sense that we would embrace our newly discovered connection to one another. I didn't know what it would look like, but I desperately wanted something to grow from there.

The meetup between my husband and half brother had given me a spark of motivation. My wheels began to spin. I decided to once again reach out to Robert after receiving no correspondence since his last email, the one stating it was nice to meet me. I thought the words from Dani Shapiro's book were so profound, so telling, that he needed to hear them also. Maybe those words could articulate that my curiosity was real. Natural.

I hit the send button the morning before Thanksgiving, hoping he'd be in good spirits. Also knowing full well that he might be surrounded by family for the upcoming holiday.

Good morning, Robert,

Hope this message finds you well.

I had originally told myself I was not going to reach out again without correspondence from you first. So forgive me for following through on an impulse.

I hope these past several weeks have given you some

time to process all of this a bit. And that you are even a little able to move from a feeling of regret into the understanding that everything happens for a reason. The reason being "me" in this case, of course.

 I'm guessing by now you've had a discussion with your sons. I am hopeful that they were able to look at the situation with grace and compassion as well. I'm sure that was a tough talk to have.

 I just finished reading a memoir similar to my situation. An author I follow who also had an eye-opening discovery after an Ancestry test. Anyhow, she shared some words in her book that I think sum up the exact feelings that I myself am experiencing. I just wanted to share them with you so that you can understand why I needed to reach out with the letter and introduce myself. It also helps explain my need for exploring your family lineage in the Ancestry family trees. I truly hope you can understand my curiosity.

 Wishing you and your family a lovely holiday season.
                Margo

I then included an image of the quote. I hoped he would understand the depth of it. I hoped it would normalize my behavior and my need to bring this all to the surface. I hoped it would open the gates of understanding a bit further. I didn't know what to expect or even what I wanted from all of it. Acceptance was all I could muster when I tried to figure it out for myself. I only wanted to be acknowledged and welcomed in some way, big or small. So as to say, "You are part of us, even if we don't know you. Even if we choose not to get to know you. You are part of us, and we acknowledge this truth."

The next day, Thanksgiving morning, I opened his short reply.

Margo,

Happy Thanksgiving to you and your family! Your message leaves me with much more to think about. Thank you!

Robert

Enter more thoughts and analysis. *What did he mean by that response? Should I have settled for the silence of crickets?*

> Grace means that
> all of your mistakes
> now serve a purpose
> instead of serving shame.
>
> — Brene Brown

CHAPTER 6

The Tangled Web

Naturally, my mind ran rampant in processing all the people and lives that would be affected by my need to dissect my buried truth. I had willingly opened this can of worms and had zero plans to keep my identity a secret. I had long fantasized about acknowledging it and saying it out loud. Wonderment had been removed from the equation, and I was suddenly experiencing myself with a sense of certainty that I couldn't explain with words. The strongest desire to know even the smallest of details surrounding myself had taken over. Like a snag in a fine piece of fabric, the unraveling had begun, and there was no stopping it now.

I had a million questions, and I wanted—better yet, needed—the answers to those questions more than ever. It felt incredibly selfish at times, leading this quest with my own heart at the helm. But I knew beyond the shadow of a doubt that I was meant, maybe even guided, to uncover this truth. This was a necessary part of the journey of uncovering the me that I am. Quite literally the "next chapter" after publishing my first memoir. I had to constantly remind myself that I had spent forty-seven years living a lie, a lie that others might have covered up and kept from me intentionally. A lie, let us not forget, that my unpredictable, narcissistic mother had drunkenly shouted at me when I was just a young child. Far too young to understand its ramifications.

It dawned on me during this unveiling that she was the only one who ever shared this possibility. If she hadn't, I would have likely exited this life never knowing the truth of who I am. I was grateful she had planted the seed. Drunkenly slurred or not, I owed her that much. I wasn't ready to make sense of it as a young girl. I wasn't meant to make sense of it until this moment. Circumstances had to be aligned perfectly for the unfolding of such a revelation, and I was now ready. *But is everyone else?* I couldn't help asking myself.

I was naturally curious about my BC father, the father who had been in and out of my life up to that point. I had spent my life pitying him. For what he had been through with my mother. For the estranged and fading relationships he had with me and both of my brothers. For his inability to show emotion the way we needed when we were so young and at any point throughout our lives. I felt deep pity for the way he depended on his mother and a series of wives to care for him. He was seemingly incapable of navigating the rigors of everyday life without a female to run his household, a strong contrast to the independence I have always exhibited. We never had a close relationship. I don't recall him attending events or performances I was in as a child. I don't recall conversations or discussions about my interests or my future. My earliest memory in life was of a time when I was three and he physically lashed out at me in a drunken rage. My thoughts immediately dove back to those early years:

Did he hold resentment toward me right from the start?
Did he know all along that I was not his flesh and blood?
Did he look at me and see another man's face?
Was I a constant reminder of my mother's infidelity?
Did his parents, my beloved grandparents, know this truth, too?

If the answer to these questions was yes, it would explain so much about my life. It would explain absolutely everything, in fact. It simply had to be the case. I wondered what publicly sharing this truth would do to him. Would it bring shock and disgust and embarrassment? Or would he, like me, feel instant relief in the truth finally coming out? Freedom from no longer bearing a lie he regrettably signed up to harbor all these years?

It dawned on me that he likely spent those initial years "pretending" to be my dad for fear of deserting or hurting me. A noble gesture. Or maybe I'm completely wrong. Maybe he just couldn't handle the shame of admitting his wife had another affair. Either way, hiding the truth would fuel his fire of resentment toward me over the years. Resentment he was certainly entitled to. I had always known he could not stand the parts of me that were just like my mother. He told me that once when I was a teenager. Recalling that explosive episode so many years later gave me chills.

"You're just like her!" he shouted, glaring right through me as he scolded me for staying out too late as a teenager when I lived with my grandmother.

And now I was realizing that he also couldn't stand the parts of me that were like my real father. The one whose sperm was responsible for my creation. My heart concluded that my BC father must have known all along.

I wondered how we would move forward from this point. Would we even be able to? We had not spoken to each other for a couple of years. I was sure even more time would effortlessly pass between us now. Perhaps no hopes for any sort of reconciliation now that I had outed the truth. My truth. His truth.

Guesswork about those days and months back in 1974, the time surrounding my conception and birth, filled my thoughts. I tried to recall the people who might have been around my parents during this era. I wondered if anyone else looked at me with the suspicion that I might belong to a man other than my BC dad. Not just any man but his dear friend who had lived right next door to him. These two men had grown up together. Same neighborhood. Same circle of friends. I imagine that added an extra sprinkle of embarrassment to this discovery.

Then I would switch gears and think of the man I didn't know, my biological father.

What is he remembering as he processes this news from so long ago?
Is he in total denial?

Did he ever once calculate the possibility I could be his child, knowing that he and my mom were together right around the time of her pregnancy?

Did he time-travel and recount the events surrounding her, calculating the days?

Surely, when my mother became visibly, publicly pregnant, he would have wondered about the timing. After the shock of this abrupt news wore off, I wondered if he could accept the truth about me.

Am I forever a product of disgust in his eyes? Of shame and resentment of his past?

Or can he move beyond that with compassion and be accepting of simply what is?

I desperately wanted him to share my belief that all things happen for a reason. And that actually, I was a pretty big deal. A pretty amazing outcome of perhaps a not-so-memorable rendezvous. I mean, what are the odds?

I was especially curious about how Robert's sons were taking this. I knew one was supportive. But I had no clue how the older son was digesting everything. Even though Tim had told my husband that he was okay with the news, I had no idea whether he'd have the capacity to actually accept another sibling or admit his feelings out loud to his dad. I envisioned him as caring and compassionate. After all, he is a father to three adult children. My new niece and nephews. Saying it out loud to myself felt so weird and surreal.

Will my brother tell his children and share the news?

Will he want them to meet me and know me? My kids? Their cousins?

Or will he be so ashamed that he'll be unable to share with anyone else?

Only time would tell.

My thoughts raced regarding my own brothers, too, the ones I had known my entire life. Reality set in that they were my half siblings. I did not have a "whole" sibling, and that meant that they didn't either. I didn't expect the news to create an issue with them, because I believe we all innately knew this was the truth of us. My oldest brother does in fact resemble my mother and all the males on her side of the family.

But my youngest brother and I are unmistakable matches for the men who participated in our creation.

My youngest brother, Leo, had known his truth for much longer than I knew mine, thanks to the candid conversations my mother liked to have with children who were too young to comprehend what the hell she was talking about. To her, kids were adults. She treated us no more gently than the friends she had in and out of our house at all times. My heart broke to think about the young boy my brother was back then. Likely no older than six or seven when she told him his real dad was a man other than the one we knew. His story was not a rumor or possibility like mine. It was one most people knew, including me. Here I was, an adult, having a difficult time making sense of my own truth now that I had proof. I couldn't begin to imagine how heavy that knowledge must have been for him to carry all those years and even now.

I vaguely remember that he met his biological father once, as a child. This man, who was also in my BC father's circle of friends, often hung out with the neighbors of my childhood home. He would occasionally be spotted on their front porch, perched right across the street from our house of secrets and chaos. My very young brother marched up to him once and blurted out what my mother had told him so matter-of-factly. However, the man made it clear from the start that he was not interested in any sort of relationship or getting to know this cute little towhead. Bitter words that carved deep scars into a young boy who looked just like him. I reminded myself how lucky I was to be processing my news much later in life, when I had the mental faculty to deal with all the emotions and the stings that would accompany it. An identity crisis was no small feat to take on, even willingly.

After the initial confirmation of my DNA test, I spent a good deal of time trying to interview any willing adult who was privy to the details of my mother's life around the time I was conceived. I had hoped her sister, my only living aunt, would effortlessly recall the facts for me now that I had presented cold, hard proof. I knew she would be cooperative and want to help me. Problem was, I was asking her to time-travel back nearly fifty years. I am sure she could hardly recall the personal events of her own life, let alone those of her sister's.

"Your mother liked to make things up. I do remember some sort of fling going on with them back then. But I didn't know the details, and your mother didn't always tell me everything," she openly shared.

The way she delivered the story led me to believe that my mom must have alluded to others that lines had indeed been crossed between her and Robert. But it seemed that her promiscuity led her nearest and dearest to perhaps "blur out the details" so as not to be involved in her tangled web of deception. In other words, no one wanted to be guilty by association.

I asked one of my first cousins to probe her father—my uncle and godfather—for any information he might recall about that time frame. Like my aunt, he was now in his seventies, and I wasn't hopeful for what he might be able to contribute.

"Yeah, your mom got into trouble with him. Your aunt sent me out in the middle of the night to go get her once. She used to babysit for them," he recalled easily. He was referring to young Robert and his wife, of course. But my uncle didn't seem too sure about the period he was recalling.

I was not having much luck and began to wonder if I would get any real leads on who might have known my truth or not.

Thoughts soon shifted to my dear, sweet grandmother. The one who took a major part in raising me during my younger years. The fact that she was not my biological grandmother was the toughest pill to swallow. I was closer to her than anyone else in my family. She was one of the only adults of my childhood who talked to me about ancestors and their way of life. She told me stories of people who were essentially no longer my people.

Did she know? I asked myself. *Did she also carry this secret with her all those years? Did she feel sorry for the little blond, green-eyed baby girl who came into this world as a product of her daughter-in-law's infidelity? Or did she know absolutely nothing about the life her son endured with his mentally unstable wife?*

I dare say, my questions about her knowledge on the subject have plagued me the most, to this very day.

She definitely knew my little brother wasn't my father's son. We had a candid conversation once surrounding this fact, though she did not tell me in so many words.

"You know, we didn't get to see Leo when he was born. Your mother kept him from us for a really long time. He was more than a year old when we finally got to know him," she revealed in a way that helped me read between the lines.

She wasn't the type to talk derogatorily about others, and she didn't want to spell it out. So I didn't make her. This was her way of telling me that my mother carried shame about yet another affair that led to her impregnation by a man other than her husband. It didn't seem to matter at all to my grandparents, however. They loved us all the same. They welcomed us all the same. I thought about how dearly my grandmother adored me all those years. If she could love my little brother, who did not belong to her son, then maybe she had given me the same acceptance in light of my secret circumstances.

All this deception was overwhelming, to say the least. My thoughts bounced from pity and sympathy to anger and rage and back again. Coming to terms with not knowing the details was something I simply couldn't get past.

I thought about my own children, my two grown daughters. They, too, were essentially being robbed of their truth. Their history. Their genetic makeup. Their identity. This was most certainly not just about me. How could I be deemed selfish when this impacted many other people? It simultaneously infuriated and saddened me to think about the number of people affected by this one little lie. I was angry that I had to be the one calling everyone else out on their behavior and the part they likely played in the cover-up.

More than anything, I wanted someone, anyone, to give me the details from 1974. I deserved that much, didn't I?

Every podcast interviewer would eventually ask me the same

question my therapist asked: "What do you want from the unearthing of your story?"

I wanted just one adult to come forward and hand me the truth. The whole truth. No matter how hard it was for me to hear it or for them to say it.

> I am out with lanterns,
> looking for myself.
>
> Emily Dickinson

CHAPTER 7

Photographs

While I spent a good deal of my time wondering how others were processing the news of the "birth" of Margo Reilly, I spent double that amount ruminating on my own thoughts and feelings about myself. I tried to intellectually fit the pieces together and figure out what the hell this was all supposed to mean for me.

Sure, there were a few days when I forgot about the ordeal completely, going about my daily rituals just as I had before I acquired this truth and newfound identity. But other days—most other days—I wished and prayed for any sort of communication. A minuscule indication of what this revelation meant for my future. I was disappointed that things were moving along at a snail's pace. Rather, things were not moving at all.

One summer evening, a whole year after learning my roots, I was sitting in my vehicle at the end of our long driveway. I was patiently parked, waiting for my oldest daughter to grab something from her car before joining me in mine so we could head out to do some shopping. I watched her stroll toward the passenger side door and open it. Her build and stature were an exact match to my husband, her father. Her gait was so much like his that it brought a giant smile to my face. I teased her and told her what I was giggling about and admiring as she took her seat next to me in the car.

Does she walk that way because she learned to mimic him? Or does she walk that way because the skin and bones that shaped and formed her told a story about the man who created her? I instantly choked up at witnessing the uncanny resemblance. Cue the waterworks.

I wondered immediately if I, too, walked just like my biological father. The desire to know was overwhelming at times. *Why didn't I pay more attention at our meeting that day at the diner?* Some days I simply didn't have the ability to turn off the curiosities and fantasies.

Later that same evening, I sat in our living room with my husband, one eye on the TV and the other on the moving pen mapping out my daily planner. Right next to the television, on a bookshelf, was a photograph of me from my first birthday.

There is very little photographic evidence of me as a child; my mother's ex-husband tossed all our photo albums into a dumpster many moons ago, but I acquired this picture when my mother passed away. It was actually a gift I had given her many years earlier. Her mother, my grandmother, was in the photo with me, posing next to my first birthday cake. I was delighted to have this memory returned to me as part of a small collection of photos I received when my mother perished, photographs she must have found at her parents' house after they died. She left them in a large golden envelope with my first and middle name handwritten on the front. There were a few other memorable items inside, one of which was my hospital baby bracelet detailing the time and date of my birth. A true heirloom. The tag that connected my place in the world to the family chosen to be mine.

This picture of my grandmother and me tugged at my heart each time I caught it out of the corner of my eye. Not just because my beautiful grandmother was featured in it and she had long since passed but also because it held an entirely different feeling now that I knew. Now that I was certain. I used to be the star of that photograph. An adorable little towhead turning one year old. Only now, when gazing at my innocent expression as I smashed into the cake and posed for the camera, I couldn't unsee it. The child in that photo, that beautiful, innocent baby girl, partly belonged to someone else's family.

My Irish genes must be extremely strong. When I look at the

picture now, I don't see myself or my grandmother. I see him, my real father, peering through my eyes and blank expression. Little did I know then that I would study every single picture of myself in the same scientific manner from that point forward. Dissecting all the nooks and crannies of my body and face to piece together where they derived from. An obsession that would grow out of control at times.

I was so curious. Captivated. Enthralled. I desperately wanted to pore through pictures of him growing up through the years so I could make further comparisons and assurances. There was no denying his nose. His eyebrows. His eyes. They were also mine.

When the Ancestry news first appeared in my inbox, one of the first people I reached out to was my first cousin on his side. His niece Leanne, his sister's daughter. Leanne was just a handful of years older than me. She had become privy to the possibility we could be cousins after I shared this rumor with her at a party during high school. Most likely the same party where I had joked with Paul. I pitched the news randomly and casually, as if it were no big deal. I didn't know her well at all but for some reason must have felt compelled to say it anyway. Maybe I was trying to fit in.

Neither of us was old enough to process the idea that it could be true. We just thought it was cool that the possibility lingered in the air. Fast-forward to my Ancestry discovery, and she was one of the first to witness my truth unfold, as she was already in the registry. One of the perks of the website—and the reason why I felt compelled to warn Robert about what was coming, as I saw my news being revealed to relative after relative—is that you can view who has opened their Ancestry notification to acknowledge the new addition to their family tree.

We messaged back and forth almost immediately. Now that we were full-grown adults with families of our own, this information became far more than a cool possibility. It meant we were, in fact, first cousins. It meant that her grandparents were my grandparents. Thinking about how much bonding and connection I had missed out on over the previous forty-seven years saddened me, but Leanne's response was heartening.

"Oh my God. I have another cousin!" she said with a welcoming tone. "This is amazing!"

At least one person genuinely felt this way about my abrupt arrival.

It was a full-circle moment to no longer have to entertain a rumor. One of the first things Leanne shared with me was a picture of my biological grandparents, Max and Doris. It was of them on their wedding day, quite young in age. I am always overtaken with awe when looking back on old black-and-white photos, even of complete strangers. But this one had the power to suck me back through a portal in time and space. Just like with the picture on my living room shelf, the investigator in me began examining every last detail of these people I belonged to. My grandparents, young and in love. I got stuck admiring the face of my grandfather Max especially. There was something there, grabbing my attention, and it only took moments before I saw plainly what it was showing me.

I quickly copied and cropped the photo so I could home in on Max's face. The features were remarkable. The ears, cheekbones, eyebrows—his facial infrastructure was a 100 percent match to that of my oldest daughter. My eyes immediately welled with emotion as I was reminded that discovering my true identity was about so much more than just me.

I frantically searched through my daughter's Facebook photos until I found one she had posted while away at college a couple of years earlier. She was in her school gymnasium, and her hair was pulled back, so it was easy to see her features. I saved it to my computer and zoomed in on her head. I then created a photo collage for comparison, with the two of them side by side, her and her great-grandfather Max. The resemblance sent shivers down my spine. It bothered me deeply to think she would have never known that she looked just like the Reillys if I hadn't taken that test. I felt more assured and validated than ever that taking the test had been the right thing to do. Shouldn't we all know our roots and where we come from?

I created a folder on my computer labeled "Reilly pics." A place that would soon become the collection site for all additional evidence I could scrounge up about who we really were. A little library I could visit when the urge to make sense of and connect the dots flooded me.

I shared this remarkable photo collage with my daughter and immediate family. We simply couldn't believe it. We were going back two whole generations, and still those roots were not only present but as strong as ever. I copied and pasted my photo creation and sent it off to my new cousin Leanne, who agreed that the resemblance was uncanny.

Prior to the uncovering of my truth with Ancestry DNA, I had spotted a few old photos of Robert Reilly floating around on social media. Funnily enough, the father who raised me was in several of the shots with him, providing more evidence that they had grown up as friends—or at least having shared many acquaintances.

Another photo I stumbled across on Facebook stood out. One I could not stop obsessing over. A group of about twenty men had gathered to pose for the shot, which I gleaned was taken in the late '60s or early '70s based on their clothing and hairstyles. There were so many familiar faces. Not only did I spot the face of my biological father, but the man who participated in the creation of my baby brother was also staring back at me. His face was an identical match for my brother Leo, just as mine was for my father's.

I wondered, with disgust, how many of the other men in the photo my mother had gone to bed with, quickly concluding I didn't want to know the answer.

Although Robert wasn't on social media, a couple of people had shared current photos of him that were easily searchable. One of those people was his granddaughter. My niece. I easily stumbled across images of her wedding day a few years prior. There was a family photo of her and her husband with the Reilly side of the family, and there stood Robert with his current wife. Each time I acquired a photograph to add to my collection, I spotted something different about him. In this one, I was once again reminded that we have the same exact nose.

Whenever I decided to take a break from the search, Ancestry would provide another perfectly timed dopamine hit directly to my email inbox. The Reillys had plenty of archived information in their database. News clippings and old black-and-white photo evidence of my ancestors showed up almost daily, preventing me from taking the pause I was convinced I needed.

Is it a sign? I would ask myself. *Am I meant to keep digging? Am I supposed to be anxiously looking for myself in these strangers?*

But the toughest picture to look at was the one that stared back at me each and every day. The one reflected in the shiny-looking glass that would never let me forget I had changed. The face I would look at for the remainder of my days. An everyday reminder of him. Of my parts of him. The parts of me I did not know.

The depth of our resemblance to one another truly made me wonder. If I could see it without any effort at all, what was it like for my parents to look at me all those years as I grew up? As I grew into the undeniable face of a Reilly?

Sure, as I've said, I look a lot like my mother. And with that comes another truth I've had no choice but to get comfortable with. My BC father had a tough time looking at me because I reminded him so much of her. And now I was curious about what Robert saw when he looked at me. I did not want to be the face that continued to take him back to the days of poor decisions and extramarital affairs. But this would likely be the case. I was the face of his past. I wondered, desperately, how I could ever make him see me. The person I had become. Not her. Not a skeleton from the past. Just a real human being searching for connection and answers and acceptance.

Some days I felt relieved and happy at finally uncovering my truth. Other days I felt nauseous, thinking that I had lived nearly half a century without this pertinent proof of my existence. Who was I?

The few biological-family photographs I had access to brought about the highest level of mindfuckery you could possibly imagine. I stared at them endlessly, demanding answers.

But the answers had yet to come.

They say a picture is worth a thousand words. And while I'd heard that phrase tossed around over the course of my life, I never expected to internalize and understand it as viscerally as I suddenly did.

> There are moments,
> when you are getting to know someone,
> when you realize something
> deep and buried in you
> is deep and buried in them, too.
> It feels like meeting a stranger
> you've known your whole life.
>
> Leah Raeder

CHAPTER 8

Breaking the Ice

I chatted more than once with my husband and close friends about what my next move should be. Should I leave everything alone and just continue to wait things out? Or set the wheels in motion by choosing to make a move?

After much ado, I decided to let the holiday season come and go before attempting to reach out any further. The holidays are a busy time for everyone, and I could count on them to pass in the blink of an eye. I told my husband that I wanted to invite my new half brothers over when the winter holiday celebrations wrapped up.

Turned out, I wouldn't have to wait that long. My half brother Paul reached out to my husband just a few days before Christmas. He said that his older brother, Tim, was ready and interested in "officially" meeting me. This news felt like a gift from above. We had seen each other in passing but never had a face-to-face conversation.

My husband and Paul would plan the get-together. It was set to happen the day after Christmas, during the viewing of the football game. This meeting was a Christmas wish come true. I wanted nothing more than to break the ice and meet my other brother in an intimate setting where we could connect on a deeper level.

We decided on my house, where we could comfortably sit and chat without the distractions of a noisy public establishment. Paul mentioned that they had something to share with me, and I wondered what it could be. Paul and I had been friends for years, so he was well aware there were never any ill intentions in the seeking of my truth. But I wondered if his older brother might be a little skeptical. *Meeting me will put his mind instantly at ease*, I assured myself. *He'll see that my intentions are pure.*

The day arrived, and I was a nervous wreck. I knew this feeling well. It was the same nervous roller coaster I bravely rode the day I drove to meet Robert. I did my best to pass the time by staying distracted. I cleaned up our after-Christmas mess, made some tasty game-day snacks, and paced my house until their arrival just before the game was set to start.

I saw a red truck pull up, which I knew belonged to Paul. I wondered if they had come together or separately. I saw only Paul step out of the truck as I sneaked a peek through our window. I was a tad relieved that he would be the first one in the door. *I'll use him as a buffer*, I thought foolishly. But as he walked in, I could see that something was off. As I grabbed some items out of his hands, he confessed that Tim would not be coming. I tried my absolute best to keep the smile on my face so as not to make him feel any worse. It was clear that he felt awkward about having to relay that message. He said Tim wasn't feeling well but also confessed that he wondered if maybe nerves got the best of his brother that morning. (Boy, could I relate!)

I told him not to worry and that I was so appreciative he was there. I meant it wholeheartedly. How lucky I was to be accepted to this degree. How lucky I was that Paul knew I had a longing and was willing to do whatever it took to help me find myself. I was more than glad for this time we would spend together, which turned into an eight-hour day of Paul, my husband, and me casually chilling out in our cozy little home.

He had brought two photo albums from his childhood. I was chomping at the bit to crack them open and get a bird's-eye view of his family life and upbringing.

After sitting and chatting away for a bit, we opened the pages so I could get a glimpse of family life through the eyes of Paul's timeline. I flipped back and forth through the yellow-tinged albums rather intently, wanting to absorb his story. All the pieces and parts. But inevitably, my eyes zeroed in on the vintage photographs that specifically contained his father. Our father.

Proof. Proof. And more proof.

It was amazing how much I could see of myself in each and every picture Robert was highlighted in. In each changing phase of his life, I could recall a stage when I looked just the same. He was a handsome man, no doubt. No wonder my mother was infatuated.

There were few photos of our dad inside those pages. But I used my phone camera to capture the ones I found, with Paul's permission. The images would haunt me. I couldn't stop looking at them for the longest time. As if I needed a daily hit to remind myself who I was and that this discovery had really, truly happened. I would later dissect them further with my husband and kids. I knew they would confirm what I was seeing so poignantly. Bits and pieces of who we are. We three girls are part of this family, this bloodline, this heritage. We might never have a chance to get to know it on a more personal level. But I sure was thankful to have a few shots to give us at least a point of reference.

Paul could never know how much it meant to me that he opened a portal into his family history that day. He even took the time to tell a few stories surrounding some of the images and was sure to clarify any unfamiliar faces so I could envision a family tree of sorts.

That day together made my heart feel hopeful. A little more fulfilled. Slightly less curious. And a lot more relaxed about trusting things to unfold the way they're meant to.

Having a little faith proved to be just what was needed.

It was New Year's Day 2022. Kind of fitting when I think of it in hindsight. Starting the year off with a conversation I had been wishing and hoping to have for several months, I joined my husband at a local club. I no longer drink alcohol but will occasionally grab a stool with my husband to chat it up with the locals.

I knew when I pulled into a parking spot that there was a small chance I might run into my oldest half brother, Tim. However, as we walked in, it was easy to see he was not there. The pandemic was still causing high numbers of infections in our area, and many people we knew were sick or staying home as a precaution. Only a small handful of patrons were gathered around the bar. As my husband signed in, I hoped he would scan the guest list to see if my brother had been there earlier. Unfortunately, he didn't think to look. As he handed the book back, I jokingly scolded him for forgetting.

Moments later, the door opened to unveil Tim walking in by himself. It was mere seconds before we locked eyes, as I was seated in close proximity to the door. He looked as if he'd seen a ghost. The awkwardness was palpable and felt exactly the same as when I looked our father in the face for the first time.

The ice had finally been broken, but it was clear by his expression that he hadn't expected to see us. Yet it was also obvious that we were both relieved this was finally going to happen. This moment was necessary if there was to be any forward movement. It was time to get the introduction over and done with.

He walked toward my husband and me, shook my husband's hand, then leaned toward me for a hug. The one he'd told my husband he would be giving me. We embraced, and I murmured something to the effect of "Nice to finally meet you!" We had seen each other plenty of times before, as we had mutual friends and establishments we frequented in our small town. But we had never had a real reason to have a conversation. Knowing we shared DNA and were half siblings made things entirely different. We were somehow a small piece of each other, and it was time to get curious.

The start of our conversation was painfully slow. I held a conversation with myself about what was appropriate or not for this first (unexpected) meeting. *What should I say? Does he want to hear the whole story?* Then, more easily than anticipated, I began to summarize the story for him. I was sure that Paul had already filled him in on most of it. But I also knew it might feel different coming straight from the source. Straight from his biological sister.

I shared with him how this knowledge was delivered to me at a young age, leading me to secretly wonder whether it was the truth. I confessed that his brother and I had joked decades earlier about this very possibility yet never gave thought to what it actually meant. Then, years later, when I was diagnosed with a rare cancer, my genealogy came into question. More than ever, I wondered about my roots. I also revealed that it was the death of my own mother that had prompted me to finally get the answers I had been quietly seeking my entire life.

We filled one another in about our families and how we would like them to eventually meet. Tim mentioned that he wished he had known sooner so we could have had a chance at a real brother/sister relationship. Unfortunately, we both knew there was no turning back the hands of time. But we still had plenty of time to think about how things might go from that point forward. It was clear that all of us were curious. Curious about each other. Curious about what would happen next. But we were also, no doubt, treading water in uncharted territory. Nobody we knew had done this. We had no example or reference point for how it was supposed to unfold. Just the uneasiness that must be penetrated and processed before we could get comfortably to the other side.

It was more of the same after finally meeting Tim: hurry up and wait.

As I've mentioned, patience hasn't historically been one of my finer qualities. My early childhood left one too many scars as a result of waiting, relying on somebody else to step up and save the day.

But the fact of the matter was, I had no choice but to wait and see what this initial meeting would mean for Tim. I imagined it was a surreal experience for him as well. To look into the eyes of someone who resembled his father to such a degree. I bet he wondered, like the rest of us, how to best process and move forward when we'd all been sucked back in time, trying to make sense of what had happened.

Will he tell his children? What will they think? Will they be eager to meet me? Will they want to know my family?

It felt like meeting my father all over again.

I cared deeply about what conclusions they would each draw about me, and Tim was no exception. I was determined not to spook anyone. I wanted to be enticing and captivating so they would naturally want to seek more of me and come to know my story.

But I also had to be clear that I was not on a quest of the secret, quiet kind. I had made a conscious choice to make myself known to the world. To reintroduce myself, if you will. And with that comes great risk. My stepping out as a Reilly would most certainly cause a buzz in our small community.

Winning over my brothers was a goal that had a deep hold on me. I suppose the fact that my biological father was up there in age made me subconsciously believe that maybe I was too late. Too late to know him on the deep level I longed for. But his sons were younger, closer to my age. And it felt like a mission for me to break this ice and forge ahead to form any sort of relationship I could with any or all of them. If we couldn't proceed as brothers and sister, then I would at least like to form deep friendships that could afford us more time together. Time to explore and share the highs and lows of our lives thus far. Time to make new, fresh memories. This was a need and ache that I would not, could not, dismiss.

The burning question was *Are they open to it? Do they feel the same?*

I fantasized about ways to bring them in closer. I longed for them to want to be my big brothers as much as I dreamed about being their little sister. I didn't have any idea what it would look like. I only knew I wanted to find out. To open the door to possibility. A new beginning. A new family experience. A fantasy I couldn't seem to shake.

> Today, I do not use this
> energy to critique
> my father or his father.
> Instead, I say,
> 'Blessed be the healthy cycle
> even though it has to begin here.'
>
> Rudy Francisco

CHAPTER 9

History Repeats Itself

Let's return to the subject of patterns. Have you ever paid close attention to the rhythms and cycles in your own life? The way you prepare your coffee each morning? The route you drive to and from work each day? The habits that repeat themselves over and over, almost without thought? We come to rely on the memory of these patterns. They are predictable. Until someone or something comes along to break the pattern, it will go on and on and on. As cliché as it may sound, history repeats in much the same way, leaving the world with the choice to either embrace or challenge the patterns.

When I began sharing the story of my DNA discovery with close friends and family members, there were extremely mixed emotions about my investigating to this degree or going any further. Many people were in favor of me seeking my truth, cheering me on to discover what was rightfully mine to know. But there were also those who felt I should carry this secret to my grave in order to protect the people and families it would involve. No one presented as neutral. Each person seemed to firmly plant their stake on one side or the other.

I have evolved exponentially through my DNA discovery. And I've come to realize that there are those who attempt to live their lives with integrity. Cycle breakers, like me. And there are those who passively keep the cycles and patterns going. Those who are willing to live out of integrity, so long as it means keeping the peace among their people.

At any cost. Even that of their own well-being.

According to the popular blog site *Psychology Today*, "A cycle-breaker is somebody who sees an unhealthy cycle of behavior in their family of origin (meaning the family they grew up in) and intentionally works to break that cycle."

I had come to understand that humans are here "to do the work." The work that will break the chains and codes that keep us stuck on repeat. I have never been a quiet person, and this experience prompted me to realize that my voice could be used to heal and inform others so they could do the same. Healing, of course, means facing the truth. Addressing the truth, no matter how vulnerable or delicate the situation may be. It certainly was no easy task, nor is it an easy task for anyone brave enough to take the leap.

Many times throughout my DNA discovery, I had to come to terms with the fact that my beloved grandmother who raised me was not truly my grandmother. Aside from my husband and kids, she was my closest human connection. Some days, I felt deep compassion for the possibility that she was trying to protect me by withholding this information. Other days, I was enraged that the one person I believed I could count on in my life would deceive me to such a degree. Furthermore, I had to slowly digest the discovery that her good friend and neighbor across the street was my biological grandmother. I will never know whether my nonbiological grandmother carried this knowledge with her in secrecy or was completely oblivious to it. But I do know one thing for certain: she would be in favor of me discovering the truth. She, too, had been blindsided by dark lies when it came to her own family tree.

In my grandmother's eleventh hour, she feared her death. She feared dying and going to heaven.

"I don't want to go there," she mumbled in a shaky, nervous voice.

"Go where?" I replied, wondering where the conversation was headed.

"To heaven. Or whatever is on the other side," she replied.

I gave her an inquisitive look. I couldn't make sense of this, as I had always believed she was a devout Catholic. But she made a confession to me during those final days. It wasn't actually death she feared at all. It was seeing her husband and sister again. She desperately wanted to avoid any reunion that might take place in the heavens above. I couldn't understand why, all of a sudden, she wanted to avoid them.

She then entrusted me with her truth, her tone alluding to a deathbed confession. My ears perked as I prepared for the impact of her words.

After my grandfather's death years earlier, my grandmother learned a gut-wrenching secret about her husband. One that made her hate him. One that made her question her whole existence as a wife and mother and Catholic. She didn't vocalize these feelings to me prior to this eleventh-hour conversation, and she didn't go into detail when she finally did, either. It wasn't like her to speak poorly about someone else.

My grandmother's sister had gotten pregnant out of wedlock back in the 1940s. In the olden days, this was highly frowned upon. It was decided that my newlywed grandparents would take the baby and raise her as their own. She would be added to their family of four, and my grandma would embrace her niece as the daughter she never had. Imagine her surprise when, decades later, several years after my grandfather's death, she learned that her niece was actually her husband's biological daughter.

So many questions bubbled within me. I can only imagine how devastating this truth was for my grandmother to face. Deceived by her own husband and sister, together. Duped through all those years to think she was doing the "right thing" by taking her niece in and raising her as her own.

Scenarios played out in my head. *Was this a consensual affair? Did my grandfather force himself on her? How did this happen?* I imagined my poor grandmother's imagination running even wilder than mine. *How could they?*

And now here I was, scratching the surface of some dark, well-kept secrets myself. History repeating. A pattern resurfacing.

I had a vivid dream shortly after the passing of my beloved grandmother. I was standing in the kitchen of my home when the phone rang. I walked over to the wall and picked up the corded handset to answer. My grandmother was on the line, calling me directly from a pay phone booth in heaven. I saw her vividly in my mind's eye. She stood behind the paned glass on a busy city corner. It resembled the city we lived in. She told me that she wanted me to know that she had arrived as planned. Our conversation was calm and casual, as if I had expected this call to come.

Then she told me she had seen "him" in passing. She was referring to my grandfather. She said he didn't know she was there, and she didn't have to interact with him, which put her at ease. I was delighted to hear this news and felt her relief. She was safe and content. She'd arrived safely on the other side. Delivered to heaven to live on without suffering any longer from illness or from those who cheated her.

My dreamed-up phone call left me at peace. I no longer worried about my grandmother, though I also never doubted for one second that she would be made comfortable when she arrived. She was a saint, after all. One of the only role models I had in my lifetime.

Recalling this memory reminded me that I had been witness to this phenomenon of history repeating itself on other occasions as well. There were times I myself was responsible for partaking. Before I understood how to "do the work," that is.

I had a huge blowout with my narcissistic mother when I was pregnant with my first daughter. We were exchanging some harsh words, and she attacked me physically. I was only a few months along in my pregnancy, but that did not stop her from lashing out. Because it turned physical, I refused to speak to her for a long time after that particular episode. Therefore, she was not included in the baby shower or birth. This was not a deliberate punishment but rather a choice to protect my family from the crazy world where she still thrived. I don't think she got to meet my daughter in person until she was about a year and a half old.

At the time, I didn't recognize the similarity to when my mother gave birth to my youngest brother and didn't allow my "paternal" grandparents to see him until he was almost two years old. This estrangement was rather perplexing to me as a child because I was always at their house. Of course, I now understand why she kept him away. She carried profound guilt and shame since he was not my dad's biological child. Unlike when she was pregnant with me, her infidelity was public knowledge during his pregnancy. She intentionally kept him away from my grandparents even though my BC dad was once again covering up her lies and deceit, playing along as his father.

It dawned on me that perhaps karma had played a role by delivering her a taste of her own medicine. It seemed lessons in infidelity and "illegitimate" children had not yet been resolved in my family's trauma cycle. *Wow*, I thought as I came to this conclusion. *History really does repeat itself. All you have to do is look for the patterns, and you will find them.*

I recalled the time Eric dropped out of college when he unexpectedly became a young father. He had enrolled on a full scholarship due to his impeccable grades and ability to learn easily. He attempted to stay the course with a new baby on the way, but ultimately, he sacrificed his potential, as life had other plans for him. He was needed at home. This scenario was all too familiar: This same exact story had played out for my mother and father just a couple of decades earlier when my brother himself was on the way. My BC father, who also had lots of intellectual potential, dropped out of college to become a young father as well. He would spend his years working in a factory to provide for his family.

I am sure it wouldn't take much effort to recall many other instances where the same scenes continued to play out through generations. It was almost fascinating to take notice of. Clearly, there were lessons that had not yet been learned. The cycles would not stop or change until someone decided it was time. That time was now. That someone was me. I couldn't bear the thought of ignoring what I knew. I couldn't bear the thought of willingly sending my children on in life without doing something to help stop the toxic, unfathomable cycles.

I knew that "doing something" involved having discussions. I knew it involved acknowledgment and processing. But how was I going to get others on board? Everyone I knew allowed shame to keep them from speaking the truth. They were comfortable living lies. They were prepared to take them to the grave. I simply could not and would not be that person.

It has always been my sincerest hope that healing myself might ultimately lead others to do the same—or at least open them to the idea that it can be done. They, too, have a choice. The questions remained, however: Would they join me? Would they speak candidly to release the lies that haunt us? Or would they continue to play the charade to protect their own egos and/or the ones they claim to love?

I desperately wanted either of my fathers to come forward with the truth. I wanted to know about the breakup of their friendship. I longed for them to tell me every last detail surrounding my conception, shameful or not. I wanted to hear how they felt in anticipation of my arrival. I wanted to know what transpired over the months that my mother carried me in her growing belly. I wondered what it was like, those first few months after my arrival here on Earth. Was there ever any sort of acceptance? Or was the response instant rejection?

I had answered these questions once or twice in my own mind. But I craved someone else's confirmation of what I had conjured. I wanted just one person to be forthcoming with information. To be the victor in my search for the real answers. The hardcore truth. No matter how much it stung.

It was easy to make a conscious decision to finally heal and save myself. I'd been forced to apply healing tactics in so many situations throughout my life. But I was coming to understand that there was far more to this mission than simply creating a road map that could save and heal me alone.

I am no fool. I know I don't have the superpowers to save everyone, nor is it my job to do so. But since the start of this journey, I have felt great purpose in healing out loud instead of quietly, without notice. Maybe, just maybe, someone around me was also ready to stop the toxic patterns. I did not want history to continue repeating itself over and over, rotting the roots of my family tree from the bottom up. I didn't yet have a concrete plan as to how I was going to conquer this mission. But sharing my story, this story, felt like the most natural starting point.

I had made an important decision: it stops with me.

A brave move that would take immense dedication, compassion, forgiveness, and, most importantly, time.

Breaking chains is not for the faint of heart.

> When you finally learn
> that a person's behavior
> has more to do with their
> own internal struggle
> than you,
> you learn grace.
>
> — Allison Aars

CHAPTER 10

The Last to Know

I find it rather amusing the lengths we will go to in order to protect ourselves. Even if it requires sheer denial of blatant truth. I witnessed this many times with my mother. Denial is an easy form of self-protection. Problem is, it keeps us from feeling or processing the necessary emotions to move through any particular event or episode.

Sure, it's normal to use this tactic in the short term. It buys us time to collect our thoughts on any given matter before we move through the process to acceptance. It becomes a problem, however, when we clench so tightly to the denial that it becomes a believable truth. Denial gives us permission to box up what happened with a pretty little bow, hoping and praying we never have to open it again. We must take caution, though. That box, tucked away out of sight and mind, can and will eventually resurface.

Have you ever been broadsided by a slew of information that immediately made you feel shocked, and then, just moments later, you questioned whether you already knew the information? Sometimes I am convinced that the truth lives buried deep within us. In fact, one of my favorite quotes from *Eat, Pray, Love* author Liz Gilbert is "The Universe buries strange jewels deep within us all. And then stands back to see if we can find them." I had to come to terms with my truth being inside me all along.

Weeks—months, even—had passed since my Ancestry discovery

on that hot August day. Yet here I was, still trying to figure out how it would all play out, especially when it came to my BC father.

I was visiting my older brother Eric for a Thanksgiving gathering a year out from my initial discovery. I confessed to him that I still couldn't wrap my head around how our shared dad would react upon learning this information, since we hadn't spoken in a couple of years. I also wasn't sure how he would find out I had gone searching for my truth. He hadn't been on speaking terms with my older brother or his family for years either.

Eric looked at me and very matter-of-factly said, "Oh, he knows."

I was puzzled. "What do you mean he knows?" I had never heard this from him before.

"They definitely argued about this when we were little. I remember. I even remember the name Robert Reilly getting thrown around, too," he offered nonchalantly.

He assured me it was an acknowledged issue between my parents that I might not belong to my dad. At least, acknowledged back in those early years.

I wondered why my brother and I hadn't had this discussion long ago.

But of course! If she was willing to throw it in my face when I was a mere child, I could only imagine the number of times she insulted my BC father with this potential fact. She was wicked in her ways, after all. Of course she used this to hurt him! Why didn't I come to this conclusion sooner?

For some odd reason, I had been trying to convince myself that there was a chance that my BC dad didn't have a clue. I had been coming up with what-ifs, giving all these adults the benefit of the doubt that no one told me because they truly didn't know it was a possibility. But I was slowly uncovering clues and facts that indicated many of them did know. Many people around me seemed to be privy to my truth. Except for me, of course.

I got nearly the same reaction when I finally had a conversation with my youngest brother. In the most recent years, we had also had an estranged and complicated relationship. I had only spoken with him a few times since our mother's passing.

I was not initially planning on sharing the news of my Ancestry results with him. He did still actively speak with our BC dad, and I feared he would run straight to him with the news. I imagined my youngest brother would take comfort in knowing he was not the only "illegitimate" child in the family. That I, too, was an outcast. A mistake. Another shameful product of my mother's careless choice to sleep with whomever the hell she pleased.

An opportunity knocked, however, during one of our rare phone calls, and I had the sudden urge to tell him what I had discovered.

"I confirmed that Dad is not my dad. I took an Ancestry test, and Robert Reilly is definitely the one." It rolled out of my mouth without effort. Each time I said it out loud, my body became lighter and freer.

He delivered a confused pause. "Wait, I thought you already knew this?" he asked.

"No. I didn't know this. What exactly do you mean by that?" I barked back at him.

But I knew immediately that he was referring to the discussion we'd had decades earlier when we were way too young to know what we were talking about. When I told him that our mother had made the insinuation and then denied it the very next day. But this by no means meant I knew anything for certain. It was just a possibility. One that no one ever spoke of again. One that got deeply buried like the rest of the scars and secrets we children were expected to box up with pretty little bows and keep for an eternity.

He then proceeded to tell me that our mother had told him all about it. Those two were toxic together and thick as thieves. He admitted he always assumed she had shared the story of the affair with me as well.

No, she most certainly did not. In fact, I got total denial when I asked her about it. As if the conversation were off-limits. I didn't dare bring it up again.

I had to explain to him that it was a deep, lingering itch that surfaced every now and then. And that the time had come to finally take a DNA test and put an end to the idea, now that she was dead and gone. I suppose I took some comfort in knowing she wasn't alive to harm me for uncovering the truth of my identity. There is no doubt in my mind that there would be suffering and consequences if she were still here.

For whatever reason, I did not press my brother further. I was so stuck on anger that I couldn't muster up the will to ask what she had said to him.

In recent years, my thoughts had tried to convince me that maybe I did belong to my BC father. He and I had almost nothing in common, but there were things that made me wonder. He had piercing, light-blue eyes. I had piercing, light-green eyes. His mother—my dear, sweet grandmother—and I had both battled head/neck cancer. Even though it wasn't the same type, I concluded that it could be more than mere coincidence since I had been mostly raised in her house.

In addition, my youngest daughter is quite musically talented and has the innate ability to read sheet music and play several instruments. My BC dad and oldest brother are also natural musicians. I was subconsciously building a case over the years that my mother's words that day could have been a big fat lie. Another embellishment or stretching of the truth, like many of the words that flowed from her mouth.

No. I definitely did not *know* anything! Or did I?

I spent far too many years trying to squash the idea out of existence and carry on as if the possibility had no relevance whatsoever. Now I wondered if I was actually going crazy. *Were there other clues? Did I have other conversations with my mother regarding this that I'm simply not recalling? Did anyone else ever attempt to talk to me and tell me about this?*

I also had to factor in the recent interviews I'd had with any adults who were privy to my parents' lives in the '70s. Not one person I approached seemed shocked or surprised by the confirmation of my biological father, and I started to feel like maybe I was the only one who didn't know the truth. It seemed my story wasn't all that special, given that no one was reacting the way I had imagined.

I had invested countless hours in getting swallowed up by podcast conversations around the topic of DNA surprises. Endless truth-telling stories about families that were rocked by news of paternity results. Mothers who claimed they were surprised or in disbelief that such a thing could be possible. My mother would not be in disbelief if she were still here. She would be getting confirmation of what her gut had known all along. Her affair resulted in a pregnancy. With me.

In some sick, strange way, I took comfort in hearing the drama and lies from others who'd experienced DNA surprises as they told their stories. Many of them were, in fact, much more surprising and twisted than the tale I had to share. Some of them had happy endings of family members reunited. Some of them, like me, told stories of continued rejection and the feeling of not belonging anywhere.

Many of the tales I tuned in to stemmed from innocent infertility issues, parents who had secretly opted to utilize sperm donors in order to conceive. They had no idea that thirty or forty years later, their child would have access to DNA testing. Many donor-conceived individuals would purchase the test out of mere curiosity. Often, these parents were still together, thinking their secret was safe, which made it difficult for the child to approach them. These stories were strikingly similar to those of individuals who had no idea they were adopted. Gut-wrenching stories of people who learned that they not only did not belong to their dad but also had no biological connection to their mother.

Being stripped of who you are in an instant is a feeling I could never capture in words. I can only summarize what those in the interviews shared. I can also confirm that this is exactly what I myself experienced:

- Time stops.
- You leave your body and have an "out of body" experience.
- You shake.
- Nothing feels real.
- You wonder how many know this truth about you and have played along in the cover-up.

- You panic about how you will ever regain your composure.
- You may experience deep depression.
- You will never look at yourself in a mirror the same again.
- You are actually someone else.
- Everything has changed. Yet nothing appears different.

At this point, you might say, "But, Margo, to be fair, you did have a clue, unlike so many others out there."

And you may be right. It's possible that it lessened the blow to some degree. But I assure you, it was an identity crisis nonetheless. Crying, screaming, rocking, laughing, raging. Every emotion that could pass through me did over the days and weeks after I got the test results. Just like all the others whose confessions I tuned in to listen to, I had to grieve the person I "thought" I was. And brace to accept the person I "actually" am.

Some lingering questions in my life now had answers: My mother couldn't love me because I was a constant reminder of her poor life choices. Her infidelity and regrets. My dad couldn't love me, though he wanted to, because I was the face of his best friend. A daily reminder of his ex-wife's running around on him.

Nobody deserves to have the truth of who they are kept a secret. In almost all cases, I can assure you that the secret is far more damaging than giving someone their truth. Healing and forgiveness can only begin when we acknowledge there is something to be processed.

My dad is not my dad, people! I was raised in the wrong family.

Sit with that for a moment. Think about what it would feel like if that news were delivered to you.

I was devastated. I'm still devastated. The time loss alone is enough to break my heart into tiny little pieces. What if these people had been in my life in some capacity or another all along? Could they have filled the family void I've felt all my life?

These questions and more would spin on a hamster wheel, taking my thoughts hostage each and every day. I had to come to terms with this new norm. The fantasies and questions didn't go away. I still fight them off as I write these chapters and feel like I am reliving the pain and confusion all over again.

The truth will always prevail. We can run from it. We can box it up and stow it away. Or we can face it head-on. The choice is ours. The real question is, are we brave enough to go first? To face the unknown outcomes so the next generation isn't forced to pick up the pieces and connect the dots we weren't willing to deal with? It's a bold choice to be the cycle breaker and break the chains of generational patterns that make families sick as a result of harboring secrets.

It was an easy choice for me to make, though. I would no longer participate. I might have been the last to know. But I would no longer be the keeper of the secret.

> The degree to which
> a person can grow
> is directly proportional to
> the amount of truth
> he can accept about himself
> without running away.
>
> — Leland Val Van De Wall

CHAPTER 11

The Power of a Book

The story of my DNA discovery continued to evolve at a disappointingly slow rate. Funny that I was analyzing the amount of time dripping by, because I had convinced myself that I didn't have any expectations for outcomes. Truth is, I did.

I was going to be okay if my biological father decided not to get to know me. I just needed to know if that was, in fact, the case. Meanwhile, precious time was wastefully ticking away. There I was, dutifully writing this book to share the raw details and unfolding of my truth, and nothing was unfolding at all. During the frozen months up north, Robert and his wife were down in Florida at their winter home. Surely he was keeping busy in the toasty sunshine, doing his best to forget that we had met in the first place. I began to convince myself that the several months he'd spent away from the vicinity (and thoughts) of me would give him the exact amount of time he needed to make a definite choice not to proceed in any way. I started to acknowledge that the metaphorical crickets I was hearing signaled an inevitable outcome.

It was a cold and frosty February, four months after my meetup with Robert and just weeks before the debut of *When the Apple Falls Far from the Tree*. Some of my family skeletons were about to be unleashed from the closet after being locked away for several decades. My intuition had confirmed to me that the time was now. About that, I had no doubt. But that didn't mean I wouldn't feel the wrath that might come as the result of sharing my thoughts and perspectives, lurking just around the corner.

My phone chimed with a notification. I considered ignoring it because my husband and I were out of town for a getaway weekend. We had just sat down to dinner at one of our favorite restaurants and placed our order. I peeked down at my phone screen just in case it was one of our children. Instead, I saw a text message from my stepmother.

I had not heard directly from her in quite some time, given that my father and I weren't speaking. But I knew she was up to date on my life, as she regularly commented on my Facebook posts—including those alluding to my book soon being ready for purchase. She was cheerleading for my hard work and making comments stating how proud they were of me. "They" referred to her and my dad. Of one thing I was sure: my BC dad would not be proud of this book. There were some very revealing parts that included him. Events that had never been addressed or talked about. The book would be a tough pill to swallow for anyone in my family, but especially for him.

I wasn't sure how to respond to her text. The human part of me felt obligated to warn her, as a courtesy, of what was about to come. So I explained in my response that I appreciated her always cheering me on. And I forewarned her that this book was a healing journey for me that was likely to hurt the feelings of a few others. She emphasized that she understood and was in full support. I felt relieved and believed she meant it. I also got a strong urge to tell her what I had recently learned about my ancestry. They didn't have any idea that I had taken a DNA test to confirm what my mother had shared with me decades earlier.

It really wasn't an appropriate conversation to have via text, but it was now or never. I opted to seize the moment and spill the beans since I had her attention and she was in a good mood.

I followed up by saying there was more healing to be done besides what was mentioned in the book. That I had recently taken an ancestry test that confirmed that my dad was not my dad after all.

Cue more crickets. She didn't respond, and I was left to wonder whether she saw the text or not. I suppose that was another downside to sharing such a bold truth in a text message.

The next morning, upon waking in the hotel, I had another surprise notification on my phone, this time from a very excited friend who said, "Yay! I bought your book! Your book is out on Amazon today!"

What?! My book sales are live? This cannot be happening!

My book release had been strategically chosen for February 22: 2-22-22. Angel numbers that mean something personal to me. But it was a couple of weeks before that, so this news was completely unexpected. Instead of excitement, I experienced panic, a loss of control. I popped out of bed and sat at the tiny hotel room table to gather my thoughts. I had to get to work advertising that my book was up for sale. It was imperative that people make their purchases using my specific links so I could bank a few extra pennies from Amazon for each book. I had not planned to spend that entire morning on social media and sending emails, but this self-promotion was absolutely necessary, even if it needed to happen sooner than expected. I got busy sharing everywhere I could. The text conversation between my stepmother and me moved to the back burner.

Several days went by, and we inched closer to my scheduled book-launch day. My husband and daughters had thrown together a small gathering and celebration in my honor. I looked forward to the official day so I could finally acknowledge and celebrate all the hard work of exporting my story over the past two years.

I was an emotional wreck. For some reason, it really bothered me that I would have no family representation at this very important moment in my life. One of my greatest accomplishments ever. In attendance, no mother or father. No brothers. No aunts or uncles. Not even cousins. Any family I had left who I spoke to lived far away. While I was grateful to my close friends and my husband's family for being there, I took full note of who was not in the room as well.

Bless my husband, who kindly reminded me during a sobbing fit that morning that my lack of a "normal" family unit is the exact reason the book had been born in the first place. Without the dysfunction of my so-called family, I would not have this story to share with the world.

I wiped my tears, knowing he was correct, like it or not. Aside from my little family of four, two nephews, and a niece, I was going to be relying on the love and support of the network I had created for myself. A solid group of friends. Not my family. Not that day. And more than likely, not ever.

And then, as I entertained my small crowd for a few minutes with a reading from the back of my book, I saw them out of the corner of my eye, sneaking quietly into the room.

It was my two "new" half brothers. My husband had invited them, and I was ever so glad he did. Their entrance perked my shoulders up. A gigantic smile spread across my face even though I'd been choked up from reading my book excerpt just moments prior. It was an endearing moment, truly unexpected and profoundly welcome. I felt honored that they were so willing to embrace me as their little sister that day, even if we had already lived out half our lives without knowing this was true. As I greeted people during the remainder of the evening, I took their presence in that room as a sign. A sign that I was shedding the skin of one version of myself and welcoming a fresh, more authentic one.

My memoir officially hit the world that day, and I felt blissful and overwhelmed at the same time. I shared away, encouraging whomever I possibly could to grab a copy and give it a read. I truly believed that anyone who took the time to read it could find some inspiration for themselves hiding inside the pages. Sales took off, and the coming days were filled with questions and comments from people near and far. It was a surreal experience, and I was glad it was finally happening. My book had been born.

Initially, I didn't give much thought to how I was going to handle sharing my book locally. In fact, I had not really planned to do so. I was eagerly chatting it up and promoting it on social media, but sharing it around town was going to be awkward, considering how many people knew my story—or at least bits and pieces of it. I would have to explain my pen name and the reason behind it. I was plagued with hard choices about whether or not to do a press release or area book signings as a local author. I was morally torn over what my next move should be. I hadn't given the area of promotion much thought beyond the initial launch. After all, the goal wasn't to make money.

Then a good friend reached out with some insight that resonated deeply with my dilemma. I felt it was a true sign from above. She said, "You need to remember that your book is going to help far more people than it is going to hurt."

It was all I needed to hear. She was exactly right. I knew this, of course, down in my core. But something about hearing the words spoken directly to me from an outside source made everything alright. All that heavy hesitation lifted from my chest, and a feeling of peace and calm swept over me. This was my calling. My purpose. The story was, and is, meant for more people than just my friends and family.

Step into it, Margo, I told myself.

I quickly arranged two local book signing events and shared my official press release with the local newspaper. I trusted it was time to allow the barriers and walls to come down. I gave myself full permission to be in the moment, to embrace what all the hard work was intended for in the first place. My mess is my message—a realization I was coming to understand more and more every day.

My first book signing was held on a Saturday afternoon in mid-March. I chose a cozy little metaphysical shop that my friend owned downtown. I set up my table area with visceral excitement, feeling like a seasoned author as I arranged my books in a twisted staircase formation on my crisp new tablecloth. Fresh flowers from the owner and my faraway friend adorned the table, making me feel even more special than I already did that day. Their delicate fragrance aligned perfectly with my demeanor and mood.

As we approached the official start time, a handful of people began trickling into the storefront. One of the first faces I noticed was that of my stepmother. I wasn't surprised by this. She had alluded through social media that she was coming. But I also felt the butterflies that come with speaking to someone after not seeing them for a fair amount of time. I reminded myself to keep the smile planted on my face and just breathe it all in. She came straight to the table and was second in line, holding several copies of my book to be signed.

I circled the table and hugged her to thank her for coming. I was genuinely grateful, as it was a snowy day and she gets around with the assistance of a cane. I like to think that, deep down, she always knew that I was "different." That I had potential to shine beyond the cards I was dealt. I give her credit for encouraging me in my endeavors throughout life.

Our conversation almost immediately got awkward after I decided to go *there*. It wasn't the time or the place to talk about the Ancestry test. This day was about celebrating my book officially hitting the world. But I also knew another chance might not appear anytime soon. As I inscribed my short message and signed my pen name in the front of her books, I leaned in close to her.

"I know Dad is not happy about this book," I whispered sheepishly.

What came out of her mouth next was shocking and validating all at once.

"Your father has always loved all of you kids. He knows he is not the father of any of you, and he still chose to love you all the same," she said in his defense.

I struggled to process what had just come out of her mouth. *All of us kids? What the hell is she talking about? All of us?* Maybe I was hearing things. I knew that us two younger kids weren't his for sure. But she was clearly including my oldest brother in this declaration, which completely threw me off. We all knew Eric did, in fact, "belong" to my dad.

"What do you mean, all three of us?" I said, frowning. "Eric is most definitely his son, and we never once thought there was any question about that."

"Well, your mother told him he wasn't the father of any of you kids when she was pregnant. And he still stayed," she said.

Time stopped. I was frozen. I had to wrap my head around the idea that my father had spent five decades believing he was most likely not the biological father to any of his three children. It didn't matter that I had a room full of people staring at me with anticipation. I was being sucked into a full-on flashback elicited by a conversation I chose to start, regretting my decision to open yet another can of worms.

"Please tell him that Eric is his son. Ancestry DNA has proven it. He's linked to Dad's entire family tree. And we knew he would be. He only took the test for me," I assured her.

I thought about my younger days. When my mother and father had but a few years together as a married couple. I thought about her lashing out at him with her sharp, hurtful tongue. The way she used to talk to me and everyone else. I thought about what it must have been like to be on the receiving end of that conversation. Being told your kid probably isn't your kid because your wife can't be trusted. Being told this three times.

My father and older brother hadn't spoken to each other in nearly eight years due to a disagreement. This was the way my family dealt with discomfort on both sides. We'd simply disconnect. There was estrangement everywhere you looked. And this coping mechanism was passed down to us kids. Suddenly, I thought I knew why my father hadn't made more of an effort to resolve the conflict with Eric. Deep down, he wondered if my brother was even his son. He knew damn well I wasn't his daughter. He knew damn well that his youngest son didn't belong to him, either. But never in a million years did I think he questioned whether Eric belonged to him. I was emotionally overwhelmed, as I hadn't entertained this scenario even once. I was so caught up in my side of the story that it was difficult to process the emotions of all the others involved.

I handed my stepmother's books back to her with a slight tremble in my hand. I was startled by the serious nature of our brief conversation, but I had to shake it off and carry on as my proud author self on that special day. I gave her another hug to thank her for coming and tabled my thoughts for the remainder of my event. I couldn't wait to get home and fill my husband in on this newfound information. He had not been in close enough proximity to hear what she had said.

I peeked out at my patient little crowd, which had formed a perfect line. A little further down the line stood my half brother Paul. I knew I could count on him for support. He truly was such a godsend through all of this. He held two freshly purchased books in his hand. My smile grew bigger when his turn at the table arrived. A needed diversion from the truth bomb that had exploded moments before.

"I need both copies signed, please. One is for me. One is for Dad," he said with smiling eyes.

I signed his first. I wrote the blanket statement I had been penning into all the fresh new copies. "Always remember, you are the greatest project you'll ever work on. ~Margo."

This statement truly encompassed the overall message of my book and seemed fitting, even for him. He is always working to improve. But I knew when I grabbed the second crisp copy that those words would not fit when addressing my biological father. No. Something else needed to be scratched permanently into the front of his copy.

I took a deep breath and exhaled as I put pen to paper.

"Dear Robert, A small glimpse into my life thus far. Anxious to see where it heads from here. ~Margo."

I grinned as I gazed down at what I had written, surprised at how easily the words flowed from my heart to the empty book cover.

"His birthday is in a couple days, and I will be giving him this as his present," my brother shared with a delighted smile.

I fantasized for a moment about Robert opening this gift. A book that his biological daughter had written. A daughter he had never known. Sharing the gut-wrenching stories of her crazy life through the years. I wondered if he'd actually read it. Or if he'd conclude that it was just too overwhelming to open Pandora's box and take a look inside at what he had missed over the past five decades.

I secretly hoped he would read it word for word so he could be assured that I was a good human on a healing journey. I hoped it would encourage him into his part in my journey. I wanted him to be proud and honored enough to want to get to know me in some capacity. I didn't expect a father/daughter relationship to bloom, but I yearned for friendship, at the very least. A connection that showed we cared about and acknowledged each other's existence.

Maybe he would read the book after receiving it on his birthday and contact me to discuss how we could move forward.

I crossed my fingers in my mind, longing for his acceptance.

I spent the remaining hour or so chatting about my book and signing copies for the locals who came out to support me. Many of the people in line were from my parents' era. I made sure to spill teasers as we talked about the next book I was working on.

"Oh, if you like how revealing this book is, just wait for the next! This book will make total sense after my next one is released," I said.

> The work we do
> on ourselves
> becomes our gift
> to everyone else.
>
> Ram Dass

CHAPTER 12

Rejection Is Protection

"Rejection is God's protection." Or so it's been said. I was beginning to understand that I might have to truly internalize this way of thinking in order to best process and accept my current situation.

I am certainly no stranger to inner work. Rejection has been a lifelong theme for me. With my mom, with my BC dad, and now, yet again, with my biological father. I am not a fool. I had rehearsed for the fact that nothing might come of gaining the facts about my biological origin, and it became clearer by the day that none of these adults were going to openly embrace this truth, sharing it for the world to see. After repeatedly asking myself how I could make sense of all this knowledge, I came to one conclusion: I had to spend more time figuring out how this new knowledge was helping me or working for me, not against me.

More than a year had passed, and there'd been essentially no progress with my biological father and very little with my new half brothers. All those initial talks of meeting other family members and getting to know each other in a family context had faded away. My hopes of meeting my people seemed to be dwindling rather quickly.

Do they need more time? I wondered. *Do I need to be more patient? Or have they already made a hard decision not to proceed?* Not knowing felt like mental torture. *Please, someone give me the answer.*

I knew it in my heart; they were all following his lead. No one wanted to proceed in getting to know me because Robert wasn't showing interest in doing so himself. But even so, I longed for my brothers to want a relationship. We were in such close proximity. We saw each other around town. Our kids were the same age. I strongly felt the cousins should know each other. None of this felt fair to me. And it also wasn't fair to my daughters. How could we be shunned by those we belong to? We didn't ask for any of this.

You would think a whole year would be long enough to draw a conclusion and move on. But I couldn't. I occasionally put out feelers to see what might happen, taking a temperature check of sorts.

I learned of an upcoming Reilly annual family reunion set to happen in July. My half brothers told me all about it one day as my husband and I chatted with them at the club. Apparently, it's an annual event in the Allegheny Mountains that lasts for days on end. They told me I should come with my family to meet everyone.

"There's tons of space. We rent several extra cabins for people who come and go and can't stay the whole time," they offered.

I had butterflies just recalling our conversation about it. My big brothers chatted on and on, laughing as they told stories about prior camping trips and shared other memories from trips past. I took great comfort in hearing their stories, daydreaming of what it must have been like to be there each year.

"But what about your dad? I don't want to do anything to make him uncomfortable," I reasoned. As far as I knew, his sons were the only ones he had confessed the truth to.

"Dad doesn't come up and stay like the rest of us. He usually only visits for one afternoon while we're up there. We can find out when he is coming, and you and your family can do a different day if that works," one of them suggested.

With those words, my excitement came to a screeching halt.

Suddenly, the event didn't sound as appealing. I was quickly reminded that we were still tiptoeing around the feelings of our father. Their suggestion that my little family show up at a different time than Robert confirmed that no progress had been made in his acceptance of me. The last thing I wanted was to meet his entire family and have him upset with everyone for organizing it behind his back, without his approval.

I knew my half brothers meant well when they brought up the reunion and that they were genuine in their invitation. But they also hadn't thought it through. Their father—*our* father—would likely not be at all comfortable with his secret from decades ago casually showing up to meet everyone. I held on to the hope that someone would share the Ancestry findings with all the others. I wanted to force the uncomfortable conversation to happen between those family members so we could just move forward already.

I spent the next week fantasizing about what it would be like to go to the family reunion. To look into the eyes of even more people who look like me and possibly my children. I imagined sharing stories about our lives and hearing about my biological grandparents, what growing up with them was like back in the day. I pictured the Reillys sitting around the campfire, happy and content. I thought of my own family of four sitting there among them. It made me smile.

Time was of the essence. I wanted to do this. I was ready. I had been ready for a long, long time. I knew the only way forward was through him. The reunion was only a week away, and I needed a plan if I wanted to make this happen.

I let a few more days pass before sending an email to Robert explaining my intentions. I wanted him to know that his sons had invited me. That they were interested in introducing our children to theirs.

> Hi Robert,
>
> I hope this email finds you well.
> I am not sure where you are at in the processing of all this. I have been in contact with your sons, who have invited me to your family's annual camping reunion. Although I would love to meet everyone, I don't want to do so without your blessing.

Please let me know how you feel about this, as I don't want to do anything that would upset you.

Thanks, Margo

I knew it was a bit forward and brave to reach out in this way. But I needed to know where he stood. I sent it off and eagerly awaited his reply, which came to my inbox four days later, after the ten-day reunion had already started. I opened his response with hopeful eyes and a racing heart.

Margo,

I am still trying to process all of this.
    It is clear my sons are doing better with the news than me.
    I will not be attending my reunion this year.
    I understand you need to do whatever is best for you.

Robert

I had been so hopeful that looking into my face that day at the diner was all he would need to want to know me better. But that simply wasn't the case. His curiosity did not match mine. Rejection once again reared her ugly head. His short words jumped from the computer screen straight to my heart like a bullet. He'd confirmed that he had no interest in embracing the truth about me and sharing it with his closest people. Even worse, it now seemed he was going to avoid his own family for fear of having to bring up the past in casual campfire conversation.

The sting of his response hurt far more than I had anticipated. I knew his sons would not proceed with the invite if and when they learned that he was not ready to entertain my family being there, and I felt the crushing of my heart yet again.

I sent a brief email thanking him for letting me know his current thoughts. I informed him that I would not attend, knowing he had not addressed his family as of yet. I felt utter disappointment that a perfect opportunity to meet so many relatives at once would come and go, that time would continue to simply march on without any change. I didn't hear more from my brothers on the matter after our initial conversation about the gathering. Their loyalty to their father was the most important thing. I understood and respected that. But I still selfishly wanted and wished for more.

I felt like a small child once again. Unimportant. Unlovable. Not worthy of a seat at the table. And after I threw myself a good old pity party, I decided maybe it was time to give up on growing these new relationships.

Days, weeks, and months passed. Before I knew it, we were heading back into the Christmas season, my favorite time of the year. Nearly a year and a half since my discovery. I was on a natural high, as I always am when the holidays roll around. I'm one of those people who starts playing Christmas music two months too early. I was joyfully distracted and hadn't given much thought to my discovery or the rejection from my biological father for some time. Then, one day, I woke up and it was all I could think about.

"I am going to send my biological father a Christmas card in the mail this year," I blurted out to my husband as we watched TV one evening.

He looked surprised, as I had chosen not to send out any cards that particular year.

"Do you think I should?" I asked, patiently waiting for his opinion. He is my voice of reason, and I knew I could count on him to be honest.

"What is your intention behind sending it?" he asked.

"I just want him to know I am thinking about him. That I wish him well. I want him to know that even though all this time has passed and nothing has happened, I am still hopeful. I feel like if I don't put it out there, he won't know that I am still hopeful," I explained.

I was grateful for my husband's question. I felt good about the answer when I heard myself speak it out loud.

"Then you should do it," he insisted.

I got up from my cozy spot on the couch and headed straight to my desk to find the perfect card. I didn't want to let the idea pass me by. I didn't want to talk myself out of doing it. It felt appropriate. I was reveling in the bliss of the holidays, and I wanted that to be evident in my message. I chose a pretty plaid card with a short holiday greeting. I then added my handwritten words:

Robert and Suzanne,

Wishing you a wonderful holiday season and a healthy, happy New Year ahead!

Margo

I sent it off the next morning without a return address. I did not want him to feel obligated to send one back to me. It was eight days before Christmas, and I wanted to be sure he received it before the holiday, before he and his wife left for Florida. I was proud of putting my intentions out there, making them known instead of doing nothing at all.

Four days later, I came home from work and began opening the mail. There are always several holiday cards in our daily pile this time of year. But I quickly noted one addressed specifically to me. A grin crept across my face, the same huge grin I wore the day I received his first email. That childlike feeling surged from the pit of my stomach.

I stared for a long while at the masculine handwriting printed neatly on the front of the envelope. He had clearly been the one to fill it out. I wondered which letters he might shape just the way I did. I studied them with curiosity, then opened the envelope carefully so I could preserve the piece of him I now had in my possession. He had taken the time to send a card in return, two days before Christmas. This was not expected. But it certainly was hoped for. It felt like a special gift. A gift of promise.

The card reciprocated warm holiday wishes. At the bottom, more evidence of him. He penned the message:

Wish you a healthy and prosperous New Year. Think about you often.

Robert and Suzanne

My eyes fixated upon the words "Think about you often."

I wondered how much truth there was to that statement. Hope flared and was restored within me. He didn't have to mail a card back. He certainly didn't have to add those extra words. But he did.

I snapped a picture of the card and envelope side by side and texted it to my husband. "Look what I got in the mail today!"

I spent the next few hours attempting to quell my excitement. I'd spent my whole life waiting for the other shoe to drop, and this day was no different. Reminding myself that Robert would be leaving in just a few days for his annual trek, I didn't want to allow myself this level of enthusiasm. The card was simply a lovely gesture brought about by my decision to make the first move after a long bout of silence. I believed his words, though. I believed he spent time thinking of me. However, even if that was true, he still wasn't sharing those thoughts with others around him, or with me. He still quietly carried the secret within him.

Despite our lack of progress, the card renewed my faith and kept my hopes alive. Was this man just not sure how to let himself proceed?

One thing was clear. By allowing myself to feel the rejection over and over and over again, the sting reminded me to focus on who I truly am.

Margo, you're no quitter, I assured myself.

PART 3

Healing the Wound

> Maybe you are searching among the branches, for what only appears in the roots.
>
> *Rumi*

CHAPTER 13

Signs and Synchronicities

You would think I would have taken the hint. But time and time again, I chose not to acknowledge it. I didn't want to. The desire and need to belong, particularly to a strong and loving family unit, remained, even as life seemed to be proving that the more I yearned for it, the further it floated away from me.

Am I wrong to want this? I asked myself. *Why isn't it happening for me? Haven't I gone through enough to be granted my happily-ever-after?* I wasn't asking for Prince Charming, for heaven's sake. I was merely seeking an adult who chose to genuinely know me. A parent figure who could accept me unconditionally, as I am, regardless of how I came to be.

The birth and death of relationships was not a foreign concept to me. Plenty of people have moved into and out of my life. Family members I'd seen and spent time with on the regular as a child were now long gone from the picture. Some friendships shriveled like a California raisin when I stepped into my life as an alcohol-free person in my most recent years.

But I was now also an experienced adult, hyperaware of the people patterns that exist. They say when one door closes, another opens. I so deeply wanted to believe that for all those who had exited my life, a replacement was just around the corner, ready to divinely fill the empty space.

Of course, you wouldn't catch me referring to this aching need. I had faith, always, that the right people were placed in my life at precisely the right time. Time changes everything, even the most solid of relationships. The ones we have with others, even the ones we have with ourselves. I was changing and morphing throughout this experience, and it was easy to witness.

For the millionth time, it seemed the universe had ordered me up a fresh set of goggles so I could look at my situation from a different angle and with at least an ounce of grace. I had been the product of an affair. Possibly a one-night stand. There was no changing this truth. This secret, forbidden encounter brought me into this world. I had no choice but to embrace the decision they made on that day, whether they recalled it or not. It created me. I exist because of it. I am on purpose. No longer the mistake I once convinced myself I was.

If you have spent your life like I have, trying to find your place within your dysfunctional family unit, then you know how difficult it is to even find yourself in the greeting card section at your local store. I was anxiety stricken each and every time I needed to purchase a card for an occasion concerning my mother or BC father.

Aside from the entirely blank options, there wasn't a single one that fit my situation. "Dad, you've always been there for me." Or "Mom, you're the best!" Nothing quite matched the awkward, strained relationships I had experienced with my parents, and I would reluctantly rummage through the available choices, hoping to find the most basic words. Words that weren't even slightly mushy and gushy, because that simply wouldn't work. I couldn't choose false phrases and accolades for parents I'd spent my life feeling so disconnected from. In those greeting card aisles, I found myself green with envy for those who could choose the loving, thoughtful sentiments my eyes fell upon. I have always been jealous of friends who held close relationships with either or both of their parents. Why couldn't I have at least one?!

I remember hearing a theory once, either in a book or on a podcast, about the "one-third rule." It argues that the people in our lives, family and friends, can be broken into three different categories. The basic premise is the reality that not everyone is in your corner, cheering you on. You have your committed third, those who are genuinely interested and actively curious or involved in your life. Next, there is the third who remains fairly neutral about your actions and endeavors. They could take you or leave you. The last third is entirely checked out from you and your interests. Don't call upon this third when you need support, because you won't find it.

This theory doesn't seem far-fetched. In fact, it's quite easy to buy into when you think of your own friendship circle. Hell, I could easily place each of my friends into these suggested categories. What is far more difficult for me is the reality that our family members fall into these categories as well. There are those you can count on. And there are those who are clearly uninterested in anything you say or do. The business of belonging becomes somewhat blurred when we attempt to view it through the lens of this one-third rule.

My therapist has reminded me, on more than one occasion, that the need to belong to a pack is innate. We are all born with it. My longing is absolutely normal. And the truth of the matter is, I finally did belong. Thanks to the internet, I belong to a group of people just like me. Seekers of true identity who also want to know who they are and exactly where they came from.

When I joined several DNA support groups on Facebook, I was quickly schooled on various terms and acronyms widely used within this community of seekers. I am now an "NPE," which stands for "not parent expected" or "nonpaternal event." In other words, a DNA surprise. There are thousands of us out there, attempting to connect the dots on our own, thanks to at-home DNA testing being so readily available and inexpensive.

Almost daily, I could expect my phone to ping and let me know that I had another Ancestry family hint to investigate. Many of them were connected to my mother's family tree. But the majority were guiding me toward my paternal lineage, which was more heavily populated within my Ancestry data. Each time a notification arrived, I clicked to follow through on the hint, hoping to find an attached photo and perhaps a glimpse of my face in people I didn't know. There was always a strong desire to feel physically connected to these people who were part of my roots. It saddened me that I would never really understand my heritage. That many opportunities for discussion had been lost.

Sure, I could research and investigate from that point forward. I could question those still living who might be willing to talk with me. But that is not the same as having candid conversations with my biological grandparents, who lived right next door to me once upon a time. There were aunts and uncles who never knew I was their niece. There were cousins I never got to hang out with. So many chances had passed me by. It was inevitable that the longing would continue. I had found yet another thing I would have to formally learn to grieve: not knowing my true roots and those missed opportunities to connect with family members who might have been sane and willing to love me all those years.

I flashed back to a childhood memory during one such bout of yearning. My best friend Sarah and I were having a good old-fashioned argument. We must have been nine or ten years old, sitting on the front porch of my BC grandparents' house. It would've been hard not to notice us. I had white-blond hair, and she had flaming-red locks. I cannot recall what had two young girls so heated and irritated, but I do remember we were yelling directly into each other's faces as we sat on the old metal glider, each trying to prove our point.

I hardly noticed when one of our next-door neighbors, Max, approached. He was a grandfatherly type who had a sweet nature about him. He took a half step up onto the open porch and gently interjected to get our attention off each other and onto him. We turned our heads sharply toward him, a bit shocked someone had sneaked up on us.

In a kind but firm way, he scolded us for wasting such a beautiful summer day on an unnecessary disagreement.

"What could two young ladies such as yourselves have to argue about? You are wasting a perfect summer's day by getting yourselves all upset. You're too young for big problems like this!" he declared.

Summertime in my small town has always been a time for fun

and adventure. We are a lakefront community, and a quick bike ride can deliver you right to the stunning shore of Lake Erie. There are also many adorable parks throughout our little city, and in my youth, it was safe to venture out to any one of them with a pack of friends to hang out for the day, unsupervised, until the sun went down.

In Max's hand, he held some dollar bills. I hadn't noticed them initially, but I quickly saw where the intervention was headed. He insisted we use this money to walk over to the local corner store for an ice cream treat so we could do what young kids ought to be doing: enjoying a carefree summer day.

We didn't hesitate to take the bait. Our frustrations, whatever they were on the blazing-hot afternoon, instantly turned to smiles as we popped up to take him up on his generous offer. Who can refuse cash or ice cream? Not us. It must have been exhausting to take life so seriously, and I am grateful he interjected to snap us back into our proper childhood roles.

And it turned out Max was actually my biological grandfather. Only I had no idea that he and the family next door were part of my true identity, my heritage, the very essence and DNA of my bones. I wouldn't come to know this truth until decades later, when he was long gone.

In hindsight, I think Max might have taken a special interest in me. Maybe it was because I was the outgoing little blond girl always prancing about in his neighborhood like I owned the place. Or maybe, just maybe, he was a keeper of the truth. A secret keeper of the lie that told my story. It pained me to think he could have known that truth and not rescued me.

All of Max and Doris's children had been raised in the very house the couple still resided in as aging elders, right across the street from my nonbiological grandparents. Their kids grew up alongside my dad and uncle as best friends from the neighborhood, chumming together well into their high school years. My dad was close to several of Max's sons. Even though he was slightly younger, he did his best to keep up with the good old boys, from what I could tell from photos and stories.

It absolutely haunts me to think of the irony of the situation.

My mother had cheated on my dad with his longtime neighborhood friend. A friend who grew up right across the street from him. The family I was raised in and my biological family resided in houses just twenty feet away from each other. While I had caught glimpses of Max and his family's comings and goings over my younger years, I would never know them on a personal level, only in casual passing, like the day Max came to rescue me from a heated debate on my grandmother's front porch. I will always be left to wonder whether any of them knew I might have belonged to them.

DNA-surprise stories can be extremely difficult to dissect and solve. But in my case, the answers were quite literally feet away from me the whole time. Ironically, the family that I looked like had watched me grow up from their porch and picture window.

I recently learned of another coincidence that I hadn't given any thought to. When my husband pointed it out to me, I could not help but thank the cosmos for conspiring to work on my behalf.

He reminded me about the circumstances of our first daughter's birth. I had been finishing up my last semester at college, and he was working as a machinist at a small local factory. We did not have a lot of money when we were starting out. My husband was searching for a minivan, as he didn't have a terribly reliable car. Most guys might have been embarrassed to drive around in a used minivan. But the thought delighted my husband, who was excited to bring his baby girl home in it. Eventually, he found a cheap one and did just that.

"You want to know something really crazy?" he asked me now, half laughing. "You know that van I bought to bring our daughter home from the hospital in? The Astro van? Well, if you can believe it, I bought that off your new brother Tim. All of his kiddos probably came home from the hospital in it when they were born, too."

"Are you serious?" I chuckled back. "That is so crazy! What a small world! What are the odds of that?"

Here we were years later, and he had made this connection while chatting with me.

I wanted so badly to remember all the hints the universe must have been working hard to deliver to me throughout my life. The signs were most definitely there. I just wasn't open to receiving them before, I guess.

Dear universe, I am ready now!

> You are the ancestor
> that changes everything
> for your bloodline.
> You are the golden light
> in human form
> brought to earth
> with a higher purpose.
>
> UNKNOWN

CHAPTER 14

Family Secrets

The reality I had started to accept was this: my story is not that big of a deal. There, I said it.

Initially, I wanted to believe that I was the only one who could possibly have a story as mind blowing and icky as mine; however, that feeling did not last long. As I joined groups, read books, and binged podcasts surrounding the topic of DNA surprises, I swiftly came to a realization: every single family has a secret. And many are far more twisted and unbelievable than mine. In fact, mine was actually fairly common in the world of DNA surprises: Mom had an affair with Dad's best friend.

It helped to know I was not alone in navigating the wavy waters of deception. I was delighted there were others who could understand what I was going through. But it was almost equally disheartening to learn that the phenomenon was far more common than any of us would like to think, especially considering those who were born and raised "back in the day." It took much less effort to keep a secret in those times, before the internet, camera footage, and GPS tracking could do the work of a private investigator. I learned that almost any given family who takes a DNA test will likely stumble across some unknown facts in their family's lineage.

One of my biggest inspirations for writing this book was listening to Dani Shapiro read her memoir aloud. Her story is vastly different yet entirely the same. Our outward circumstances are not at all alike, but our identity crises and quests for answers are strikingly similar. My identification with that yearning was what made me feel connected to all the DNA-surprise stories I would eventually stumble across and absorb. We are all seekers, seeking ourselves, the bits and pieces that don't add up or make sense. Longing to fill the empty spaces within our beings we know are there.

Her book showcases the first story I came across that validated what I was feeling. What was happening to me. The words on the page spoke to me, I suppose, the way the Bible speaks to religious people. The more I read, the more I engaged with my deepest, longing self. It felt like a manual of sorts. Everything she so eloquently articulates is exactly what I was experiencing. I wanted to capture my raw feelings as she had. I knew that others would also likely take comfort in knowing they are not alone. So I began to faithfully record my feelings as the situation developed over the days and months after my discovery.

Life would now be forever marked by "before I knew" and "after I knew" the truth of me. And it would come with schooling on the vast world of DNA and how it works. An ongoing education for me, as there are still many facets I cannot wrap my head around.

In fact, this entire incident had me perpetually ruminating on all the "befores and afters" I could reference throughout my life. So many milestone markers clearly capturing the start and end points of seasons I'd lived through. Before and after my chaotic childhood. Before and after weight-loss surgery. Before and after a cancer diagnosis and recovery. Before and after sobriety from alcohol. And now, before and after I learned my biological truth.

Growing up, I expected milestones to come along. After I graduated college. After I got married. After I had kids. I never in a million years saw this milestone coming. Yet here we are. Another "before and after" that poignantly marks the course of my life path.

It also made me think about the precursors or nudges that evoked these wanted or unwanted turning points. My weight-loss journey is a great example. Most people who battle weight issues know it is a lifelong journey. But a pivotal moment stopped me in my tracks and forced me to address it. I was at an eye exam and had my four-year-old daughter with me. As I sat in the doctor's chair, my daughter pointed to my stomach and said, "Doesn't my mommy look like she's gonna have a baby?"

I was embarrassed when the doctor pretended not to hear her, but I was also awakened. That was the day I decided enough was enough, and I was going to seek medical help to get my weight gain under control. It was a reminder that I had let my true self go. I had given up, given in.

I eventually realized that this same sort of self-realization had urged me to buy the $79 Ancestry test. An internal nudge that simply and gently said, "It's time. Denial stops here."

I hadn't the slightest clue of the ramifications of spitting into the test tube that day and casually sending it off. I was simply seeking a yes or no answer in regard to my brother and me. Instead, I unleashed the floodgates of a brand-new identity.

I think so many of us are clueless about those potentially life-changing little kits that cost less than a hundred bucks. The only thing I knew for sure was that the results could tell me whether I shared DNA with another individual. After my initial urge to make the purchase, I didn't spend a single moment investigating the website before checking out. I plopped the kit into my virtual cart and paid, all within a minute.

When the kit arrived in the mail, I don't recall reading any instructional literature other than how to actually complete the test: Open vial. Spit a billion times until you reach the fill line. Seal it up. Send it back in the provided pre-paid box.

I vaguely recall a disclaimer I was supposed to acknowledge when I received my results via email. But I obviously took no time to peer it over, given that the screen shouted, "Results ready!" To this day, I have no idea what that disclaimer entailed. I just wanted my facts and ignorantly scrolled right on past the fine print.

Curious while writing this book, I logged on to the Ancestry site to see if I could find hints of that disclaimer I had unknowingly agreed to—only to find paragraph after paragraph of details on their legal and privacy sections. Some of it is obvious, and some of it is presented in terms beyond my understanding. One line in particular stood out above the rest. The line everyone should take heed of if they proceed in testing themselves:

"You may discover unexpected facts about yourself or your family when using our services. Once discoveries are made, we can't undo them."

My initial thought when seeing that disclaimer was *Wow, they really should consider putting that in bold letters on the actual product box!*

It's amazing, the amount of information that can come from a simple at-home DNA test kit, and it was all fascinating to me. I was schooled on so much more than whether or not I had a full sibling. Of course, not everyone was thrilled with the information delivered by my test results.

"She can't know anything for certain. She doesn't have any DNA samples from me," my BC father told my youngest brother upon hearing that I had taken a test to confirm he was not my actual dad.

"Dad, she doesn't need your DNA," my brother attempted to explain to a thoroughly confused man.

My Ancestry DNA tree had all the proof I needed to confirm who my actual father was. There was no need to rule anyone out. I understood his confusion, though. I, too, was blindsided by the plethora of information that could be provided by such a quick and simple process. I had a good laugh and a similar conversation with my husband and daughters about this very thing. I had purchased them each an Ancestry test kit as a Christmas gift the year of my discovery. I wanted to link them up to my tree so we could put an end to any questioning about who we are. I wanted my girls to go through life with facts, not lies or rumors, guiding their way.

My husband quipped that he was not going to take his test.

"I'm not spitting in that thing. I spent several years in the Army, and who knows what could have happened during that time! I'm not taking any chances," he said matter-of-factly.

My grown girls and I giggled at his lack of understanding.

"Dad," my youngest daughter interjected, "I hate to break it to you, but my sister and I are taking the test. And if you have any unknown children out there, they are going to link up to us as half siblings. We don't even need your DNA to figure that out." Insert more laughs.

His frozen expression proved he had processed her words.

"Ugh. I guess you're right," he said, releasing the puzzled look from his face. I imagined my BC dad had likely come to the same conclusion after giving the matter a little more thought.

No, my story is not all that rare. At first, it felt like a dirty little secret that could only happen to me. But as I listened in on dozens, maybe even hundreds, of podcasts where DNA-surprise stories poured out of soul seekers like me, my story felt like no big deal at all. I even felt a little fortunate that I'd always had a tiny inkling that I didn't belong. Many others were completely stunned by their truth.

The common thread throughout every story, however, was the lies. Big or small, each and every one of the stories began with a lie. Or, at the very least, an omission of the truth surrounded by lots of denial. Some lies were based on great intentions, like those surrounding individuals who were conceived through donors. Parents who desperately yearned for a child but were unable to conceive on their own. They turned to unregulated sperm banks in secrecy, never expecting their truth to be known or shared. Little did they know, it was common for one donor's sperm to be used to impregnate many women, and these children would grow up connected by DNA to half siblings, resulting in sheer shock on all sides.

Many lies were based in shame. Mothers who got pregnant at an early age or out of wedlock and were forced to put their newborns up for adoption. Young women who were raped by family members and didn't have the heart to tell anyone. My heart broke as I listened to a young woman who had discovered she did not belong to the dad who raised her. She pressed and pushed her mother for information. Her mother soon fell deeply ill, and it was revealed that she had been raped by her own uncle and never told her husband—or anyone else, for that matter.

Most of the lies were based on willful deception. The classic story of infidelity. A perhaps regrettable choice. One-night stands or lengthy affairs of the heart. Women who thought their secrets would follow them to their graves. These stories are not only the most common version of a DNA surprise, they are also likely the easiest to solve, as the clues in these cases are usually pretty obvious once you go looking for them. This, of course, was the case in my story as well.

I was grateful I didn't have to go digging. I was lucky that my puzzle was fairly easy to piece together. Yes, I was still quite disappointed that relationships hadn't blossomed with my new family. But I'd had the opportunity to meet my biological father, nonetheless. So many never get to experience that connection after discovering their truth. I at least got to have a conversation, even if it was a once-in-a-lifetime opportunity.

I was also rather fortunate that my ethnicity had not shifted drastically from what I had been raised to think it was. I always knew I had a good amount of Polish and Irish heritage. I did think I was far more Polish than I actually am. Turns out, according to several of the DNA sites I have since uploaded my information to, I am 50 to 60 percent Irish. In many DNA-surprise stories I've heard over the past two years, the person involved was shocked to discover that not only were they an NPE, but they also had an entirely different ethnicity than the one they'd spent a lifetime identifying with, doubling the blow.

A great epiphany arose from listening to and identifying with those DNA-surprise stories: there was still more work to be done. Secrets make us sick. I had seen it play out in the family I was raised in. I had heard countless stories outlining how it happened to others as well. I had come so far and realized so much in my personal forgiveness and acceptance journey. Yet there it was. That tiny itch that would not be ignored.

It was time to not only face my own personal family secret, the one I had given the power to hold me hostage for far too long, but also heal from it. I knew more about myself than ever from this DNA discovery. And now it was time to confront the part of me that kept this wound alive and thriving.

> You cannot heal
> what you hide.
> You cannot heal
> what you ignore.
> You cannot heal
> what you cover.
> You cannot heal
> what you avoid.
>
> Josefina H. Sanders

CHAPTER 15

The Way Out Is In

It became crystal clear that I had some major self-reflecting and forgiveness to tend to. One of life's hardest tasks is calling yourself out on your own bullshit.

I am no hypocrite. My life isn't perfect. My marriage has had its ups and downs like everyone else's. There were choices I made that I'm not proud of, and one incident in our nearly forty years together took time for us to heal and recover from. I love my husband and family too much to rehash any of those details here. But I will say this: If you hold judgment about someone or something, the universe will come along and hand you a big old life lesson to help you through that. If you have the audacity to think or say, "Not me. Not my family," you should do the work to change your belief that you are exempt from such things.

I previously held many judgments against my parents, particularly my mother. Her lifetime commitment to promiscuity made me cringe. What kind of monster puts themselves first to the degree that she did? What kind of monster cheats on the one they love and puts their family in jeopardy?

I held tight to those judgments—until the day I found myself in the exact same position.

It took years of intentional mindset work and forgiveness to get to the other side of how and why such things could happen in my own "perfect" life, a result of my own choices and actions. And even though it went down well over a decade ago, it is hard to make sense of any of it.

In retrospect, how I found myself there was no mistake. It was part of the grand plan, whether I wanted to admit it or not. That is not to say I am brushing it off like it was no big deal. It was a terribly big deal and a huge mistake on my part. But I learned a whole lot about myself in that short period where I lost my sense of self, a lesson I clearly needed.

It can, and often does, happen to anyone. No one is exempt from the temptations of life.

I could write a whole book on this chapter's topic alone, but that is not the purpose of sharing my DNA story. However, understanding and forgiving my mother, and now myself, was an integral part of my journey. We both needed compassion and forgiveness. I cannot be ashamed to admit that I, too, am human and made a mistake once upon a time. I cannot change my past. I can only grow and evolve from my experiences, both good and bad.

I think author Brianna Wiest sums it up best in her book *The Mountain Is You*:

> Sometimes, you have to figure out who you aren't to realize who you are. Sometimes, you have to understand what a good relationship isn't to understand what is. Sometimes, you have to walk alone to understand the value of your inner circle. You have to be rejected to appreciate acceptance, and you have to get a little lost in order to understand what path is really yours. Sometimes, you have to identify everything you don't want before you can claim everything you do.

I have never understood those words more deeply than I do today.

Life is certainly not linear. As my first memoir detailed, my life has been one big roller coaster ride, every single dip, turn, and plunge shaping the person I am proud to be today. I can't say that I would change a thing.

My husband granted me forgiveness. Not because he had to but because he knew I had temporarily lost my way. He knew, with certainty, that when I said I was sorry and it would never happen again, I meant it. And I did.

I have to spend the rest of my life dueling with the guilt around my choices from so long ago. Something that time can heal but not change. But I will admit, that chapter of my life helped me to understand my mother more than ever. I finally saw that, like me, she spent her whole life wanting to belong. To be chosen. Putting all her energy into seeking what she could not give herself. We were on parallel journeys.

Unlike her, I thankfully learned my lesson after one mistake. This was when and where I truly began to awaken and do the work of healing my wounds. This inner reckoning began long before my sobriety from alcohol sped up the healing process. I finally understood that the encounters and relationships in our lives are meant to be mirrors, reflections that allow us to see ourselves more clearly. To take note of what needs to be embraced or let go.

Although I don't understand many of the lessons that are hand-selected for us to live through and then process, I do believe forgiveness is a journey within ourselves as well as a necessary and purposeful part of our personal evolution.

Forgiveness. It's a mighty word with grand implications. Sometimes misunderstood or misused. Difficult to swallow. And often avoided for as long as possible. At least, this was the case in my experience. It's so much more than a word we throw around in conclusion that everything is suddenly "all better." It's hard, daunting work, done straight from the heart. An emotional tango and quite possibly one of the toughest tackles of my adult life.

I believe that, as humans, we often avoid using or honoring this word for fear that we are letting someone off the hook for what they have done, ourselves included. For fear that honoring forgiveness means we are okay with what happened. Let me explain how this couldn't be further from the truth.

Iyanla Vanzant is quoted as saying: "Forgiveness is not about the other person or what they did. Forgiveness is for you and about you."

It took me decades to understand the powerful and necessary purpose of forgiveness, an inner tool I'm still learning to navigate and apply every day. My ancestry journey handed me a bundle of truth with layers upon layers of lies, cover-ups, shame, and denial wrapped tightly around it. The only way I was going to understand my worth and purpose on this planet was to get to work. I had to apply what I had learned about forgiveness and how it can help heal any broken soul. I knew one thing with certainty: I was done feeding the lie. No more keeping it wrapped up tightly. It was time for its unleashing.

When we are in denial, we choose to ignore or look the other way. When we make that conscious choice to stuff it down, out of sight, out of mind, we also make the choice to pass it on to the next generation. And thus, the pattern continues. I wanted nothing more than to cease the patterns and traumas that showed up so rabidly in my family dynamics, and I began to understand the role I could play in bringing an end to those cycles that hurt us over and over again.

I consider forgiveness to be one of the greatest gifts we can give ourselves.

We must first understand that it is the tendency of our "monkey mind" to keep us stuck in the past. Reliving and rehashing even the smallest of negative moments and scenarios. Holding us hostage, never allowing us to let things go.

Forgiveness is the solution, the way forward. It's a daily commitment to doing the work necessary to keep our mental state as healthy as possible. It's an action we consciously bring forth in order to quiet or squash repetitive patterns of victim mentality. It's a full understanding that what happened, happened, and it's in the past, where it will remain forever. That only we have the power to move forward from it, and that we *can* move forward, no matter how difficult it seems. It takes a great deal of self-discipline to let go of the harmful scenarios we have let take over our minds for so long. But this form of surrender, or letting go, will bring about a level of peace that your truest self has sought for as long as you can remember. Staying caught up in the endless cycle of negativity affects us both mentally and physically.

When we do the work to get past these triggering events, whether on our own or with professional help, we reap the benefits of a healthier existence all around. We free ourselves from the chains of the past when we process, forgive, and choose to let go. We sleep better. We have less anxiety. We feel lighter. We live and love the way we are supposed to. When we actively begin to heal the things that hold us back, we welcome the path of growing and evolving. Forgiveness is one way to quantum-leap our gains.

I want to be absolutely clear that forgiveness is not condoning a situation or behavior. It doesn't mean the other party was right or justified in their actions. Forgiveness is not turning a blind eye, pretending it never happened at all. Instead, it's understanding that no one can go back in time and change what did occur. It's making a conscious commitment to move forward and not ruminate on the past.

It's imperative to remember that forgiveness is primarily about you. It's about your ability to process and heal and move on as opposed to wallowing in what-ifs. It's making your state of mind your primary focus.

Given my past experiences and hurts, I was more than familiar with this process. Hell, I should have it mastered. I spent four whole decades learning to forgive myself and others around me for various wrongdoings. My ancestry journey was simply another huge mountain I was meant to crawl. Another peak I would eventually conquer. I had already forgiven those who took part in my lost childhood, and I would now have to embrace forgiving any and all who had taken part in keeping the secret of my conception. And now that the truth had been publicly revealed, I would also have to forgive those who continued to deny me my place in the world.

Life doesn't play fair. However, I subscribe to the notion that whatever happens *to* us happens *for* us. In tough times, this idea can be hard to appreciate and comprehend. I am not referring to tragedy here; I'm talking about the highs and lows of everyday life. Guilt and shame are challenging emotions to face and process. However, none of us can avoid experiencing them. As humans, we will all err and make mistakes. Ultimately, it is what we take away from the lessons that will define who we are and are not.

Although my initial response to the information on my computer screen was relief, my findings brought about a slew of emotions I still work through now and again, even two years later. I wanted to be angry with the people who pretended they didn't know. I wanted to blame those who kept me from knowing a family who had been right there in my visual field for my entire life. I wanted to excuse their choices as being a direct result of my own unworthiness. I purposefully chose to proceed with forgiveness.

Forgiveness is the work of a lifetime, a core belief and a reckoning you will come to rely on if you want to move forward into healthier thoughts about yourself and those around you. It trains your brain to become more empathetic to people and situations. To understand that each of us has our own perspective and take on any given situation or outcome. Empathy can be rather hard work, as it requires you to put yourself in someone else's shoes, so to speak.

I had to face the fact that my biological reveal was not just about me. I had to consider the life-changing consequences that could have come about had the truth been known back then. Marriages would have come into question. Friendships would have been severed. Neighborhood bonds would have been broken.

After careful thought, I came to realize that had all happened anyhow. Nobody had acknowledged the truth of me all those years ago. But the damages and evidence were certainly enough to prove that something had gone down between the two families. That "something," of course, was me.

Taking the test set the ripple into motion. Others would now be affected by my opening of Pandora's box. Emails would notify other relatives of my landing on their family branches. Discussions and questions would be prompted, like it or not. As much as it haunted me to know that I was the direct reason for all these things, I also felt relieved. I physically felt the lies surrounding me lose their power. Each time I told another person and shared my truth, I felt liberated. Lighter. More real than ever before. I became accepting of my truth as I saw others able to handle it.

Sure, many were shocked and surprised. But equally as many were not. After the initial disappointment, I found comfort in their lackluster response to my news. I was born during the '70s, after all. Should we really be surprised by any of this? Life was seemingly one big, endless party back then.

I didn't know it at the time, but forgiving my parents, all of them, was the key to fully forgiving myself. My DNA discovery made me feel more human than ever, and I finally learned to love and accept myself as I am. Flaws and all.

> The final stage of healing
> is using what happens to you
> to help other people.
>
> Gloria Steinem

CHAPTER 16

Be the Person You Seek

No address. No directions. Yet it was as if our rental car were being led by a magnetic force, delivering us precisely to our destination. I could hardly believe my eyes when we effortlessly found what we were looking for.

"That street sign said Willow Creek," I blurted out. "That definitely feels familiar."

"Yeah, because we live next to a winery called that," my husband laughed.

"No. I am being serious," I promptly interjected, staring intently forward.

We were on a family vacation in Orlando, Florida. My adult daughters had convinced us to take one last trip as a family of four before our eldest daughter gave birth and officially crowned us grandparents. We had originally planned this trip for the spring of 2020, but it was canceled when the pandemic closed down our world. A few years later, we felt compelled to make it up to them before everything changed and our attention shifted dutifully to the next generation.

The weeklong agenda would include a few visits to the beach and a day or two at the Disney parks. I hadn't been to the central part of Florida in seventeen years. Our last visit there was the one and only time we ever took our children to meet Mickey.

I confess, I also had a secret agenda that needed tending to since we would be in that particular area.

Florida, specifically Orlando, holds some of my most severe childhood trauma. It's no wonder I've never had any real interest in returning. I wanted, however, to honor my daughters' longing to return as a family at least once more.

Just ten miles down the road from our vacation villa sits a house responsible for some of my deepest scars. The house of horror I was kidnapped to as a small child by my mother and her husband. The one my brothers and I came home from school to, only to find her attempting to take her own life with a razor blade. Though we lived that hell for just over six months, it felt like an eternity at the time. Just the thought of it put a lump in my throat and nausea in the pit of my stomach. Still, I knew what I had to do.

I couldn't put into words my need to take this step. It just seemed timely, a box I needed to check on my healing journey. I didn't have any clear expectations of how things would go or exactly what purpose this would serve in the long run. I only knew with certainty that it was necessary to proceed.

I asked my family to take a ride back in time with me. To search for the house I remember being located on a small man-made lake right in the center of a town just outside Orlando. They willingly agreed, knowing I was already set on the idea. We hopped in the car and followed the main highway that would lead us into this little town.

I soon realized that there was no need to search, as the very first street we picked to drive down delivered me straight into my past. When the house came into view, I knew this trip was about far more than creating new memories with the ones I love. It was also very much about shedding and releasing some of the old ones. I'm not sure what I expected to see or feel, but my healing journey had so far prepared me to be wide open to experiencing whatever needed to come.

There it was. Nestled on the corner lot, sitting directly across from the man-made lake I had remembered. Much smaller than I recalled, having aged forty years. The surrounding area no longer the pristine neighborhood it once was, the house looked rough. Real rough. Much like the memories trapped inside its walls. We drove by several times to snap photos, even parking at the corner like undercover spies at one point. I was amazed that although it had aged, it remained exactly the same. Same exterior color. Same Spanish-style stucco wall leading to the front door. Same tree in the middle of the front yard that I playfully tied my youngest brother to as a little boy, subjecting him to practically being eaten alive by red fire ants.

I didn't get immediately emotional. Rather, I felt like I was looking at a movie set. Like when you visit a museum and see props from famous TV shows or movies. It looked staged, fake, like it should have been roped off to keep people from poking at the relics. I was revisiting a distant chapter of my life. I imagined the interior as I stared at it. I had brief flashbacks of empty rooms, lacking furniture and anything else that ever made it feel like home.

More than anything, I paid close attention to how I was feeling. I had prepared myself for pure disgust, an emotion I spent way too many of my childhood years festering in. I assumed a feeling of disdain for all the adults in my life would rush over me. The mother who dragged us there. The father who couldn't find us there. The stepfather who brutalized our mother daily there. I also thought of my new biological family, who might have saved me from this life in the first place if only they'd known the truth.

But that wasn't my experience at all. I surprised myself, as I so often do these days.

It wasn't pity or deep sorrow that washed over me, nor did I have a need for forgiveness. That work had already been done. There were no flashbacks of the people or episodes that occurred inside those walls some forty years ago. In fact, it seemed I couldn't recall them in any detail if I tried.

Instead, I was overcome by a sense of release, a huge weight lifted from my body, my bones. A peace and calm that I'd been getting acquainted with over the past few years. An awareness that I was learning to master the art of letting go. I immediately recognized the voices in my head that had played on repeat when I was a young girl. They sounded very familiar. Too familiar.

No one is coming to save you.
You are strong.
You will survive this.
You will be better because of this.

They were hard words to hear as a nine-year-old. They were still difficult to digest as a grown adult. The difference was, I understood and believed them now. In that precise moment, it didn't matter where my feet were physically planted. I was there for the lesson. The reminder to stop seeking someone who was never coming. All these years later, I had still secretly been hoping to be a rescued, chosen little girl. Only now that longing was linked to a completely different family. A family that doesn't even know me—one who may choose not to.

I wasn't led there to forgive my mother, as I originally fantasized. I had been attempting to validate my feelings of lovelessness. My not-enoughness. And instead, I was greeted by that trusty wake-up call I can always count on. The blatant reminder that I am the only one who can or will ever give myself that level of love.

It's me. I am the person I seek.

Nobody spoke as we drove back to our condo, as I silently held on to those revelations for a good long while. I honored them. I validated them. And then, like so many other things in my life, I surrendered them and let them go.

It was time to stop seeking. No more searching for parents to love me and choose me. That search was over. I cannot find something that never belonged to me in the first place. It was time for radical self-acceptance. It was time to banish the judgment and analysis I wanted to apply to all things in hopes of making a shred of sense out of them.

I also firmly decided I would no longer allow childhood scars to dictate my choices in life. Florida is a beautiful place with lots to offer. If my family wants to visit one of the vacation capitals of the world, I will graciously go along. The wounds of my past will not stop me.

We go through life witnessing love stories. Most little girls grow up secretly wishing for the epic Cinderella fairy tale. But what I've come to learn in my half century of life is that love stories encompass so much more than the intimacy between two adult lovers. Love stories occur between a mother and child. A father and child. A grandparent and child. Between siblings. Between friends.

And just like the love stories and fairy tales we admire, some of them, the lucky ones, have happily-ever-after endings. And just as many of them crash and burn.

One of the toughest lessons I've learned involves the understanding that some people are only meant to be in our lives for a season. We think parents are forever. We think siblings are forever. We think spouses and children are forever. But we have no control over the time we are granted together. We are not promised forever with anyone.

Even harder to grasp is that sometimes, the death of a relationship comes far before the physical death of one's body.

I had desperately wanted my DNA surprise to be a love story. The kind where biological fathers and families embrace their newfound member with open arms and love. The kind where relationships gel instantaneously, as if they had existed all along. The kind where the past has no place in overriding the beauty of the present moment. The kind where planning future days ahead is all that matters.

My DNA surprise did not unfold like a love story, despite the hopeful feeling it initially held. And my once-upon-a-time neighborhood served only to remind me of my resilience, my amazing ability to love myself when the adults in my life were incapable of doing so.

Two quotes have deeply resonated with me since the day I stumbled across them. The first: "Be the person you needed when you were younger." That is quite a task since there were countless unfilled seats at the table of my upbringing. I do, however, feel that it has always been an underlying thread. A tenet of my identity is to be a better person each day.

The second quote also rings loudly in my soul: "Teach what you yourself need to learn." This quote is directly responsible for the book you are reading right now. If my healing journey can assist anyone else in making sense of their mess, then I have shared my story for all the right reasons.

Each day, I feel the joy and pangs of my evolution, loud and clear. There simply is no idle time, no moment that isn't making itself known to me. I'd love for there to be some sort of end in sight. But I have come to realize and accept that will never be the case. Not for me. Not for anyone, I don't think. And that is actually a beautiful thing.

No matter what your path leads you to, no matter what challenges and happy times you face, you'll feel that constant need for self-acceptance. The embracing of all your parts and all the places they come from. All your experiences that create and shape you. It's all part of the package, the gift you are to the world.

Shortly after this revelation, I decided to ask my biological father for an actual paternity test. I had run into my half brother Paul at an outdoor event, and he made a remark about me connecting to his family tree. At that moment, I wanted to squash any blurred lines regarding my place in his family. I thought maybe Robert needed proof. Maybe he needed to see it on paper, spelled out in black and white. I convinced myself that it certainly couldn't hurt to help him along in the acceptance process. I shot off an email.

Hello Robert,

I hope this email finds you well.

It is hard to believe it has been almost two years since I took the Ancestry DNA test and made my discovery. It was validation for me, although it still left some blurred lines.

When we met that day, you questioned whether you should take a test or not. At the time, I did not see the necessity. But I have since changed my mind. I think a paternity test would clear up any misconceptions or possibilities.

I am going to become a grandmother in the next few weeks. Our firstborn will be giving birth to a baby girl. Now, more than ever, I can see why the medical records component and true family heritage are so important. I want to be 100% certain when passing information down to my daughters and their children. No more blurred lines.

I am hoping you would be willing to do a paternity test, at my expense of course. This would be private and would not be linked to the Ancestry website or family trees created there. It would involve going to a lab site in your area for a swab test, and I would do the same. (We do not have to go together.) A professional lab will compare the swabs and confirm if we are biological father/daughter or not.

In the past two years, I have asked for nothing from you. My intention still remains to just have the truth I am entitled to. I am not looking for anything more than confirmation. Please know, however, that I am open to some sort of relationship if you should ever change your mind in the future.

Please let me know if you will be willing to participate. It would truly mean a great deal to put any "what ifs" to rest and know with certainty moving forward.

Appreciate your time,
Margo

As I'd become accustomed to doing, I waited patiently for his email response. Within a week, he respectfully agreed.

There was no need to search out a lab site. A week or so later, a lab technician went to his home to swab his cheek. She then drove a mile or two down the street to where I was parked and waiting for her to do the same to me. She assured me the results would be delivered in the next week or two.

I met with my therapist via a video chat the next day and told her about my recent request for the paternity test. Naturally, she asked me why I suddenly felt the urge to have one done.

"I feel like maybe he has doubts. Like maybe he needs to see an actual piece of proof that he's my biological father instead of taking my word for it," I explained.

Per usual, she fired back her spin on my request.

"Do you think maybe it might be for you, Margo? Do you think maybe you are the one who needs that piece of paper?" she asked politely. She set my wheels spinning, and I gave her a perplexed look.

She continued, "You do realize that paternity paper will be the closest thing you will ever have to a correct birth certificate? It is the only proof you will ever have of who you are."

She was exactly right. I needed it, too.

I am Margo Reilly. Then, now, forever.

> You will never be able
> to escape from your heart.
> So it's better to listen
> to what it has to say.
>
> Paulo Coelho

CHAPTER 17

Grieving What You Never Had

Today I attended the funeral of a best friend's mother. Seventy years young, she sadly died after a nasty battle with pancreatic cancer. A true matriarch. A devoted wife, mother, and grandmother. She spent a lifetime perfecting her role with those she served and loved on a daily basis.

While her daughter-in-law sobbed through the eulogy, I attempted to focus on the humorous and touching stories she shared. As the tears dropped from her eyes, a waterfall began to well up in mine. I wept with deep empathy for the loss she was feeling. But I wept for another reason, too. One that had nothing to do with the woman we were paying tribute to that day.

Even at the celebration of my friend's mother's life, the ceremony sending her off to a better realm, I found myself drowning in jealousy and envy.

This woman was the epitome of a "mother's love." The way it's supposed to be. The way my girlfriend knew it to be. A special bond that I would never in my lifetime come to understand or experience. Hearing these touching memories made me long for it all the more. My friend's display of suffering and grief was proof that their love went deep. I wondered selfishly, *Why wasn't I chosen to be loved in such a way?*

When my mother passed, I prayed for healing and forgiveness for her. I asked ever so politely that she be granted a loving experience in her next lifetime, knowing full well she must have suffered something terrible in this one.

My attendance at the funeral cracked open a wound I'm all too familiar with nurturing and healing. The mother wound. The wound I have spent a lifetime trying to accept and make sense of. The one that led me to uncover my father wound. My sibling wound. My family wound. The wounds that run deep within me, shaping who I am. The wounds that consumed my thoughts, even as I sat paying homage to a wonderful woman who had passed away too young.

I suppose I shouldn't have been at all surprised that a funeral service would cause these emotions to surface. To come bubbling up once again, as they often seem to do.

The death of my friend's mother also made me think about my own adult daughters. I wondered if their pain and loss would run as deep and profound for me when it was my time to depart. Since they, too, were granted the deep knowing of a mother's true love.

I felt shame for allowing my own hurts, longings, and traumas to fill my mind that day, but there was no sense in trying to ward off those feelings. They were all-consuming, an out-of-control, spiraling roller coaster I've found myself loosely buckled into one too many times.

I knew my girlfriend was wholeheartedly grateful for the fifty years she was raised, loved, and lifted by her sweet mother. But part of me wanted to grab her, shake her fiercely, and scream, "Do you have any idea what I would give to feel the love and loss you are bearing at this moment? Do you have any idea how lucky you are to know what a mother's love feels like?"

Suddenly, I was that little girl again. Little Margo. Longing to be loved. Longing to be chosen. Longing to be noticed. And I was in the middle of a fucking funeral.

"Does it ever end?" I asked my therapist during the following visit. Fortunately, I had an appointment scheduled that I didn't know I would so desperately need. "I have done so much work. I have forgiven all the things."

She was quick to remind me, "No. It doesn't end, Margo. It just looks a little bit different each and every time."

On the morning of the funeral, I had taken the day off to be with a dear friend in need of comfort. What I didn't know was that someone else wanted in on the grieving that day. Sitting in my car, preparing to depart from the service, I closed my eyes and grasped the steering wheel. I then looked at myself in the rearview mirror for what felt like hours but was likely only a minute or two.

I saw . . . myself.

Mostly, I saw the look on my face, the one that confirmed that the work was far from done. Another day, another wound-opening reminder.

Look, I would love nothing more than to tell all those who are in a similar place that it gets better, but that would only be adding to the lies. It doesn't get better. It does get different.

Maybe, like me, you have spent your entire life following and accepting breadcrumbs from the ones you love. Maybe, like me, you have come to a point in your life where you want to stop setting the bar so low. You want and deserve more. And I agree with you. I really do. But hear me out.

What if those breadcrumbs we have been tolerating all these years led us down a deliberate path to finding, loving, and accepting ourselves for who we truly are? Preparing us for the fact that we may never have the answers? And also—and this is important—making us realize that not having those answers doesn't prevent us from being a "whole" person? We are whole when we don't need the external parts and pieces to be responsible for who we ultimately become.

The burning question at the end of every discussion or interview with someone who has learned identity-changing revelations is "Are you glad you know your truth? Would you do it all over again?" I have listened to hundreds of people answer this question, both with jubilation and with tearful, gut-wrenching regret. Some of us get happy endings. Some of us get more rejection and devastation. I very much wanted my story to have a beautiful, happy ending. I am still holding on to that hope.

Even though I no doubt subjected myself to more rejection and grieving, I cannot and will not regret finally discovering who I am. It is my birthright. Not one person in this world has the right to keep that truth from me, no matter the circumstances. I understand this truth may be of no significant benefit to me in this lifetime, but knowing my genetics, lineage, and authentic health history may very well come into play for my children or grandchildren someday. For that, I will forever be grateful.

I will continue to grieve what I never had. I will do the work so that future generations may benefit from not living the lies my family chose to hide or outright bury.

It's true that this work is hard and draining. It's a brave choice to go through some deep stuff in order to come out the other side a healthier, more healed person. We have to acknowledge that we have, in fact, lost something, and lost opportunities can hurt as deeply as the loss of someone we love. Instead of ruminating on the loss, we must make a conscious choice to process it and move through it. We do this by acknowledging that our feeling of loss is real and valid. We might find comfort in a person or therapist who will take the time to hear us out so we can understand the value of our thoughts and feelings surrounding the loss.

This is a good time to consider joining any of the many groups whose members are navigating and processing the same situation. There is a profound connection that occurs with those in a similar position, a connection that can help lead us to take action. For those of us going through a true identity crisis, we are tasked with reconstructing that identity. While our external self may appear no different, our inner world has crumbled, and it needs to be reassembled with tenderness.

While processing my grief, I am reminded each day of one important thing: I am Margo Reilly. Then, now, forever. I will embrace getting to know and love myself for the rest of my days here on Earth. I will proudly share my story with all the family and loved ones who choose to accept and love me and all my broken, imperfect, reassembled pieces.

I wish this for all of you as well. Love yourself enough to do the work necessary to heal. We are all healing from something.

At every book signing opportunity, I write, "Love yourself most. You are the greatest project you'll ever work on." There are no truer words, and I mean them with all my heart.

I believe we can change the stigma that surrounds DNA surprises. I believe we can help prevent the sickness that comes with family secret keeping. It takes voices, advocacy, and out-loud discussions. It takes community. It takes people like you and me to speak shame out of existence so there can be space to let the healing process begin.

> I forgave you for an apology
> I was never given
> because my closure was never
> tied to a single one of your words.
> It was dependent upon
> my willingness to let go.
>
> Morgan Richard Olivier

EPILOGUE

It's December 2023, two years and a few months since finally confirming and acknowledging the truth of my existence. I recently found myself making a deal with the universe, yet again, to help me gain clarity.

I made an ask. Ask and you shall receive, right?

I was still trying desperately to make sense of my findings. Years and years of yearning and hope had left me confused and tired. So I spoke my wish out loud to the powers that be.

"If I am meant to continue to pursue a relationship with my biological father, have him send me a Christmas card. This will be my sign that something, anything, was meant to grow from gaining my truth about him."

Each day throughout the month of December, my heart would skip several beats as I approached the mailbox, knowing I had made this critically important and specific ask. Anytime I pulled out an envelope with no clear return address, I paused in wonderment. Inevitably, I would crack each open to reveal no prize inside. No special words penned in nervous yet perfect printing. Just warm holiday greetings from a person who already loved my family.

The previous Christmas, I had sent him a card, and he mailed one back. But this year, I didn't send one. I didn't want to force things. I wanted any sort of next move to come genuinely from him.

Christmas morning came, and my little family started to pour through the doors for our morning tradition of gifts and brunch. With the new baby granddaughter in tow, there was simply no time to think about my own wants or needs. Our holiday morning was magical and perfect. Abundant blessings all around. At that moment, there was no selfish need or desire for anything more.

But later that evening, when the house was cleared and I was left alone to recap the day in my mind's eye, I was reminded. Reminded of my ask to the universe. I had to come to terms with my answer. No card. I closed my eyes that evening in bed, reminding myself that I'd had enough. It was time to stop asking for more.

When I woke the day after Christmas, I walked down our staircase and smiled at the aftermath still visible in our living room. Gifts scattered all around. The glow of the tree I thoroughly enjoyed while sipping my morning coffee in peace and quiet. A short time later, I noticed the mail carrier on my front step, earlier than usual. When he walked away, I opened the front door. The freezing cold took my breath for a moment, seemingly preparing me for what was to come.

I reached forward to pluck the one piece of mail from my oversized mailbox. The return address immediately grabbed my eye. It was from him. My requested card from Robert had arrived. The day after Christmas. But it arrived.

I took in the neat handwriting that spelled out my name and address on the front, confirming he had once again filled it out himself. I carefully opened the envelope so as not to rip the perfectly penned writing. I read the message inside over and over before showing my husband the gift I had just received. He gave me a big hug, knowing what this meant to me. Ask and you shall receive.

"Well, you asked for a Christmas card," he said, chuckling. "You didn't specify a timeline for when it had to arrive."

I hopped on the computer and quickly typed a brief email to Robert, thanking him for thinking of me at the holiday. I didn't receive a reply, and I didn't need one. I had the card. The card I had asked for.

Once again, I was trapped in the vortex of possibility, or what my therapist refers to as mindfuckery. Apparently, you can count on the holidays to get your emotional wheels spinning.

That spinning lasted until St. Patrick's Day, when I would be granted another opportunity to keep a little faith about connecting with my biological family.

I sent a friendly text to my two half brothers. It said, "Happy St. Paddy's Day to my two Irish brothers from another mother." I thought they'd get a good laugh out of it on a day meant for good times and laughs. They were quick to reply, and before I knew it, I was looking down at an invitation on my phone.

"We are all over at Uncle Pat's house. Why don't you guys stop by?"

Mind you, I had woken up that St. Patrick's Day hoping we might randomly run into any one of the Reillys out and about, proudly celebrating the wearing of the green. But I never in a million years expected an invite to an intimate family gathering. My husband and I looked at each other and both knew this was a golden opportunity to break the ice with a few more family members. We eagerly accepted, and I soon found myself on my uncle Pat's doorstep. Heart beating through my chest, smile stretching across my face. *Holy shit.*

Inside, I immediately spotted some familiar faces. My brothers, of course. An aunt and uncle I had already had the pleasure of meeting up with. And two uncles I hadn't seen in decades. Their faces were familiar, but they no longer belonged to the men who used to live next door to my grandparents. They were now the faces of my uncles, and I wanted to study them. I did my best not to make my curiosity embarrassingly obvious as I sat at a table among my people. Well, a good chunk of them, anyway. My biological father was still down south for the winter. And my aunt Julie wasn't feeling well enough to attend that day.

Everyone was warm and welcoming. Nerves instantly left my body. My uncle Nick's wife, who has the same name as me, made casual conversation. She and Uncle Nick weren't privy to all the prior discussions. I wasn't quite sure what they knew and didn't know, so I did my best to answer their questions as they came. I tried to keep it brief since most of the others in the room had already heard the details of how and why this all transpired in the first place. They were quite surprised to learn that I had sat down with Robert and that he had done a paternity test at my request. What may have been merely rumor among the family was now confirmed. There I was, in the flesh, proving my place at the table. My oldest half brother requested a family photo before we were allowed to exit. I was honored and thrilled to be part of it.

When we left that evening, everything felt surreal. *Did that really just happen?* I could not wipe the smile off my face. You would have thought I'd just hit the lottery or something. I was so damn grateful I had sent that text earlier in the afternoon, the text that got us invited to my biological family's most sacred holiday.

A day or so later, I sent a friend request to my newfound aunt Margo. She immediately accepted and sent a note saying that they were delighted to meet us. I replied with an apology for how awkward the situation must have felt to everyone involved. She assured me that was not the case.

"Not awkward for us. We thought you were so brave and strong to come forward with your story. The Reilly family is very genuine and kind. We hope to see more of you guys."

I also learned several days later that my biological father had received the St. Patrick's Day picture on his phone. My oldest half brother texted it to him.

It made me feel so loved and accepted to know Tim had carried out that gesture. I had secretly hoped that one of them would.

That day, I felt like a stake was placed in the ground. *She is part of us.*

I look forward to meeting more of my family members. Hearing the stories of my roots. Introducing my daughters to their cousins. Giving myself the gift of truth and belonging in whatever form is meant to transpire. It is long overdue. I know not everyone may feel the way I do, but I will continue to show deep love and gratitude for those who are willing to welcome me and my family in.

My DNA discovery story is far from over. But I have surrendered the need to try and control it. I have accepted that my ending is written in the stars, and that is where I will look for direction from this point forward. Come what may.

APPRECIATION

Fifty years ago, the universe welcomed a bouncing baby girl named Margo. The powers that be said on that day: This one, she will be strong. She will endure hardships and longings that no child would choose to experience. But we will give her the strength to persevere. Life will throw her many curveballs. But we will give her the bat to swing. She will question her identity and purpose over and over again. But we will eventually allow her to awaken so that she can make sense of it all.

Most importantly, we will give her a lifelong companion. A husband who will enter her life when she's a mere thirteen years old. He will be her strength. Her constant. He will share his family. He will show her what unconditional love looks and feels like. He will give her the space to heal, grow, and transform. He will do all this with compassion, patience, and encouragement. He will give her two daughters to love and adore and be proud of. Together, they will create the family she always longed for.

I cannot thank my husband enough for the love and support he has given me. I am grateful every day to have experienced his unconditional love through all my chapters. He is most certainly at the top of my blessings list. Without him, none of my evolution as a human would be possible. Although I sometimes want to smother him while he snores at night, he is my favorite person. Thank you for being my rock.

And a very special thank-you to my therapist, Katie. I am grateful to have reunited with little Margo all these years later. Collecting and owning the various parts and pieces of myself is still a work in progress, but I am blessed to have your guidance for the journey.

RESOURCES

BOOK WRITING

Elizabeth Lyons, publishaprofitablebook.com
Cindy Childress, cindychildress.com/getmybookstarted
Azul Terronez, authorswholead.com
Gabby Bernstein, gabbybernstein.com/bestseller-masterclass-waitlist/
Emma Mumford, emmamumford.co.uk/authors/
Andrea Owen, andreaowen.com
Amy Ahlers, wakeupcallcoaching.com

PODCASTS

Elizabeth Lyons, *Write the Damn Book Already*
Mary Adkins, *The First Draft Club*
Matt Briel and Laruen Vassallo, *Publish & Prosper*
Dani Shapiro, *Family Secrets*
Alexis Hourselt, *DNA Surprises*
Don Anderson, *Missing Pieces-NPE Life*
Lily Wood, *NPE Stories*
Eve Sturges, *Everything's Relative*
Julie Reisler, *The Youest You*
Dr. Michelle Barr, *Loving What's Next*

BOOKS

Sheri Salata, *The Beautiful NO*
Dani Shapiro, *Inheritance*

Eve Sturges, *Who Even Am I Anymore?*
Jamie Kern Lima, *Believe IT*
Libby Copeland, *The Lost Family*
Martha Beck, *The Way of Integrity*
Brianna Wiest, *The Mountain Is You*
Chrysta Bilton, *Normal Family*
Lindsay C. Gibson, PsyD, *Adult Children of Emotionally Immature Parents*
Julia Cameron, *The Artist's Way*
Kim Strobel, *Teach Happy: Small Steps to Big Joy*

www.ingramcontent.com/pod-product-compliance
Lightning Source LLC
LaVergne TN
LVHW042249070526
838201LV00089B/80